D0929794

Understanding
JUAN GOYTISOLO

UNDERSTANDING MODERN
EUROPEAN AND LATIN AMERICAN
LITERATURE

JAMES HARDIN, *Series Editor*

volumes on

Ingeborg Bachmann
Samuel Beckett
Thomas Bernhard
Johannes Bobrowski
Heinrich Böll
Italo Calvino
Albert Camus
Elias Canetti
Céline
José Donoso
Max Frisch
Federico García Lorca
Gabriel García Márquez

Günter Grass
Gerhart Hauptmann
Christoph Hein
Eugène Ionesco
Milan Kundera
Primo Levi
Graciliano Ramos
Erich Maria Remarque
Jean-Paul Sartre
Claude Simon
Mario Vargas Llosa
Franz Werfel
Peter Weiss

UNDERSTANDING

JUAN
GOYTISOLO

RANDOLPH D. POPE

UNIVERSITY OF SOUTH CAROLINA PRESS

Published in Columbia, South Carolina by the
University of South Carolina Press

Manufactured in the United States of America

99 98 97 96 95   5 4 3 2 1

Library of Congress Cataloging-in-Publication Data

Pope, Randolph D.
    Understanding Juan Goytisolo / by Randolph Pope.
        p.   cm. — (Understanding modern European and Latin American
    literature)
    Includes bibliographical references and index.
    ISBN 1-57003-069-3 (alk. paper)
    1. Goytisolo, Juan —Criticism and interpretation.
I. Title. II Series.
PQ6613.079Z834   1995
863'.64—dc20   95-11606

CONTENTS

EDITOR'S PREFACE

Understanding Modern European and Latin American Literature has been planned as a series of guides for undergraduate and graduate students and nonacademic readers. Like the volumes in its companion series, *Understanding Contemporary American Literature*, these books provide introductions to the lives and writings of prominent modern authors and explicate their most important works.

Modern literature makes special demands, and this is particularly true of foreign literature, in which the reader must contend not only with unfamiliar, often arcane artistic conventions and philosophical concepts, but also with the handicap of reading the literature in translation. It is a truism that the nuances of one language can be rendered in another only imperfectly (and this problem is especially acute in fiction), and the fact that the works of European and Latin American writers are situated in a historical and cultural setting quite different from our own can be as great a hindrance to the understanding of these works as the linguistic barrier. For this reason, the UMELL series emphasizes the sociological and historical backgrounds of the writers treated. The peculiar philosophical and cultural traditions of a given culture may be particularly important for an understanding of certain authors, and these are taken up in the introductory chapter and also in the discussion of those works to . which this information is relevant. Beyond this, the books treat the specifically literary aspects of the author under discussion and attempt to explain the complexities of contemporary literature lucidly. The books are conceived as introductions to the authors covered, not as comprehensive analyses. They do not provide detailed summaries of plot because they are meant to be used in conjunction with the books they treat, not as a substitute for study of the original works. The purpose of the books is to provide information and judicious literary assessment of the major works in the most compact, readable form. It is our hope that the UMELL series will help to increase knowledge and understanding of European and Latin American cultures and will serve to make the literature of those cultures more accessible.

J.H.

CHRONOLOGY

1931	Born January 5 in Barcelona, the third son of José María Goytisolo and Julia Gay.
1935	Birth of brother Luis, who will also become a noted novelist.
1937	Father ill with pleurisy; he remains bed-ridden for four years.
1938	Mother killed March 17 during an air raid over Barcelona.
1948	Enters the University of Barcelona.
1952	In the fall lives in Madrid, enjoying bohemian life.
1953	First trip to Paris.
1954	*Juegos de manos* (*The Young Assassins*) is finalist for Nadal Prize; it is published by the end of the year.
1955	*Duelo en el paraíso* (*Children of Chaos*). Meets Monique Lange and Jean Genet.
1956	Six months of military service. First trip to Almería. In September starts living with Monique Lange in Paris.
1957	French translation of *Children of Chaos*. Works at Gallimard as a literary consultant.
1958	*Fiestas*, *El circo* (The Circus), and *La resaca* (The Undertow).
1960	*Campos de Níjar* (*The Countryside of Níjar*) and *Para vivir aquí* (To Live Here).
1961	Travels to Cuba. Publication of *La isla* (*Sands of Torremolinos*).
1962	Returns to Europe. *Fin de fiesta* (*The Party's Over*) and *La Chanca*. Returns to Cuba during the missile crisis with the United States. *Pueblo en marcha* (A Country on the Move) first published serially in the Cuban newspaper *Revolución.*
1963	Returns to France. Visits Algeria and Spain.

1964	Father dies.
1965	Visits the Soviet Union and spends the summer in Tangier.
1966	*Señas de identidad* (*Marks of Identity*).
1967	Travels in the Sahara. *El furgón de cola* (The Caboose). Brief trip to Cuba. Visits Tangier and Marrakesh, where will maintain an alternate residence to Paris.
1968	Travels to the Middle East.
1969	Visiting professor at the University of California, San Diego, fall semester.
1970	Travels to Mexico for publication of *Reivindicación del conde don Julián* (*Count Julian*). Visiting professor at Boston University for fall semester.
1971	Edits the first number of the journal *Libre*. Spends fall in New York.
1972	Teaches at McGill University in Canada. Edits *Obra inglesa de Blanco White* (Works in English by Blanco White), with extensive introduction.
1973	Teaches at New York University during this and following years.
1975	Death of Franco. *Juan sin tierra* (*Juan the Landless*).
1977	*Disidencias* (Differences of Opinion).
1978	Publication of *Libertad, Libertad, Libertad* (Liberty, Liberty, Liberty), collection of articles related to Spanish politics.
1980	*Makbara* (translated to English with the same title) and *Crónicas sarracinas* (*Saracen Chronicles*).
1982	*Paisajes después de la batalla* (*Landscapes after the Battle*).
1985	First volume of autobiography, *Coto vedado* (*Forbidden Territory*), a best-seller in Spain. Receives the Europalia literary prize.
1986	*En los reinos de taifa* (*Realms of Strife*), second volume of autobiography.

1988 *Alquibla*, series of television reports about the Arab world.

    Las virtudes del pájaro solitario (*The Virtues of the Solitary Bird*).

1991 *La cuarentena* (*Quarantine*).

1993 Travels to Sarajevo and publishes reports in the Madrid newspaper *El País*; these collected in *Cuaderno de Sarajevo: Anotaciones de un viaje a la barbarie* (Notebook from Sarajevo: Reports from a Trip to Barbarism). Publishes *La saga de los Marx* (The Marx Family Saga).

ACKNOWLEDGMENTS

This book is dedicated to all the readers of Juan Goytisolo. I would like to make their path of understanding shorter and easier than my own was. I first became interested in Goytisolo's work when, reading *Count Julian*, I found myself profoundly puzzled and disturbed. More than twenty years later, I am still moved by *Count Julian*, but I believe I now understand it better.

Goytisolo's novels are complex and challenging. I do not wish in this study to explain them and make them simple, but instead to show how they work their magic and why they matter. In the intervening years since I first read *Count Julian*, I have taught Goytisolo's texts frequently and talked endlessly about them with many good friends. I would like to thank my students at Dartmouth, Vassar, and Washington University, especially Ethan Bumas, for the many insights they have shared with me, as well as the participants in two National Endowment for the Humanities summer seminars for college teachers I directed at Washington University. Their courage to spend a sweltering summer in St. Louis complemented the enthusiasm with which they read Goytisolo's autobiography. I also owe thanks to the National Endowment for the Humanities for a fellowship that allowed me to complete this study.

Without my conversations with other critics and without reading their work, I could hardly have understood Goytisolo. I owe special thanks to Bradley Epps, Javier Escudero, John Kronik, Linda Gould Levine, Angel Loureiro, Gonzalo Navajas, Joseph Schraibman, Paul Julian Smith, Robert Spires, and Michael Ugarte. For my knowledge of the period, I am grateful to many enlightening discussions with Malcolm Compitello and David Herzberger. I also wish to thank Sara Castro-Klarén, who encouraged me to write this book and has always been a wise interlocutor and admired friend.

My most faithful reader and best critic has been my wife, María-Inés Lagos, whose intelligence and equanimity have contributed greatly to my work.

Thanks are due, above all, to Goytisolo himself, who created the works I study in this book.

A NOTE ON CITATIONS AND TRANSLATIONS

Page references are given in the text for all citations. For works by Juan Goytisolo, references followed by a page number are to published American translations. At the first mention of each work by Goytisolo, I give the Spanish title, followed by the title in English, in italics if a translation is available, in roman type if it is not. In subsequent references I only use the English title for all translated works.

The bibliography at the end of the book provides publication information for the first editions of Goytisolo's work and a selection of related studies to which I refer.

Understanding
JUAN GOYTISOLO

CHAPTER ONE

Introduction

Biography

In his novels, travel books, and essays, Juan Goytisolo examines aspects of his own self. His roles as Spaniard, son, brother, writer, man, and consumer have given insight to his examination of his nation, family, literature, sexuality, and culture. His is a constantly questioning intelligence, sophisticated and well informed, a mind characterized by a preference for experimentation and heterodoxy and an intolerance for complacency. From his first works, his style and ideas have been polemical, becoming progressively more complex and playful. In Spain and abroad, readers have reacted passionately to Goytisolo's satire and provocation. Readers are challenged by the complexity of his presentations and interpretations of his biography. Furthermore, Goytisolo does not allow readers to stay removed from problems presented. In Goytisolo's books we, the readers, are part of the problem. We are urged to understand ourselves through these works, to face the hidden sides of our personalities and uncover what we have suppressed.

On 5 January 1931 Juan Goytisolo was born in Barcelona. His paternal family roots were not in Catalonia. His great-grandfather had emigrated in the mid-nineteenth century from the Basque region to Cuba, where he quickly made a fortune in the sugar cane industry. He built a magnificent house in Spain, not in the Basque region but in the Catalan capital, Barcelona—the second of a series of geographical displacements designed to create a new self, more powerful and more successful. Juan Goytisolo would reverse his great-grandfather's displacements, moving away from Barcelona and social standing, identifying himself instead with the dispossessed and the marginal. Goytisolo's great-grandfather was named Augustine, as was the bishop of Hippo who wrote one of the foundational Western autobiographies. Saint Augustine's *Confessions* (398) strongly assert the doctrine of original sin and the human heart's longing toward purity and salvation. Great-grandfather Augustine's creation of the Goytisolo family fortune by exploiting black labor in the

1

paradisiacal tropical island of Cuba in the mid-nineteenth century is Juan Goytisolo's original sin, an inborn inheritance he has felt the need to redeem through a life of searching and discipline. After Augustine's death, the family sold the *ingenio* in Cuba, and the eldest son, Antonio, moved to Barcelona where he, his wife, and nine children lived from the income on his investments. Without productive activities, the family steadily descended to a respectability without affluence.

At the time of Juan's birth, his father, José María Goytisolo, was the manager of a small company, Anónima Barcelonesa de Colas y Abonos. He had studied chemistry, had an interest in ecology, and designed unsuccessfully many different scientific experiments to increase agricultural production. He married Julia Gay in 1918. Their first child, Antonio, died of meningitis when he was seven years old. Their daughter, Marta, was born in 1925, followed by sons José Agustín (born in 1928), Juan, and Luis (born in 1935). The three brothers would become writers: José Agustín a poet, and Juan and Luis primarily novelists. The family kept a house in the country, vividly described in many of Luis's novels and in Juan's autobiography. The stage was set for an idyllic childhood that promised a happy relationship between Juan and the world until three momentous events disrupted his life: the Spanish civil war (1936–39), his father's illness, and the death of his mother. In his writing Goytisolo has returned frequently to the pain he suffered as a child.

In 1938, during the civil war, his mother died, a victim of a Nationalist air raid over Barcelona. Years later, when he was a university student, Goytisolo would understand that the troops of Francisco Franco, whom his father supported, were responsible for his mother's death. Retroactive redefinition is a frequent procedure in Goytisolo's writing. The child may well have been happy and believed his parents were loving and powerful, innocent, and safely established in a nurturing society. Only later did the man understand the price paid for his private child's paradise by others—slaves in Cuba, defeated Republicans, and exploited workers in Barcelona. This unsettling experience, when a state of contentment proves to have been based on illusions, makes Goytisolo skeptical of any claims of self-evident happiness or perfection, whether the claim pertains to the nation, the political party, or the heterosexual couple.

His mother's death is first recounted in a brief autobiographical portrait Goytisolo contributed in 1975 to a collection of essays about his work. He excuses himself, in the first paragraph, in italics and within parenthesis, for speaking of himself in the third person, attributing this mannerism to common usage. Characteristically, he reflects here on the strictures that constrain not only living a life but also telling a life. The third person will later reappear in his extended autobiographical writings, indicating, by the gap between the *I* of the narrator and the *he* of his younger self, how different the writer has become from the person he was in earlier years.

The autobiographical evocation begins with a date: 17 March, the day when his mother went to Barcelona to visit her parents, herself still little more than a child in the center of a Barcelona in the midst of war. While she was shopping, a bomb dropped from an airplane killed her but spared the bag in which she carried the presents she had bought for her children: a sentimental novel for Marta, the elder sister; adventure novels for José Agustín; an illustrated book of stories for Juan; some toys for Luis. Whether these presents were in fact bought by other grownups, to console and distract the children, or by the mother herself, they are remembered as humble monuments of an almost invisible life. Ten years after the brief autobiographical portrait of 1975, Goytisolo further developed his mother's figure in the first volume of his autobiography, *Coto vedado* (*Forbidden Territory*). He marvels at her adaptation to the demands of a conventional bourgeois marriage, where she is a calm, elegant, and efficient housekeeper, mother, and wife. Goytisolo finds in her a deeper and more complex reality by compiling a list of her favorite books, mostly in French, including works by Proust, Gide, and Anouilh, and reveals that she even tried her hand at writing a novel. Goytisolo embraces her passion for reading and writing as his inheritance, one he will set against the original sin of the Goytisolos. Thus, he gives us a moving recollection of an almost unknown mother but also indicates the preferences of the son, for whom family life is "pedestrian" and "mediocre" (43) while literature offers a deeper life with "hiding places, havens for rest and meditation, and pleasant, protective shade" (43).

His father, José María Goytisolo, held a management position in a factory until the war, but in 1937 he became sick and bedridden, presenting to his son Juan the picture of a decrepit and almost repugnant invalid. When he recovered his health, already a widower responsible for four children, he invested part of his capital in a series of experiments in chemistry and agriculture but they floundered because of his inadequate administrative skills and poor judgement in choosing partners. While tracing Juan's conflicting relationship with authority to his mixed feelings toward his father would be reductive, the same pattern describes his attitude towards his father, institutions, and country: an ideal is not met; claims of authority are frail; misunderstandings are numerous and profound, and yet the unavoidable relation is intrusive and persistent. Beyond rage and rejection, there is a profound affection for his father that flickers between annoyance and love. The child Goytisolo was disappointed by his father's sickness, the adolescent was condescending about his father's sadness and repeated business failures, and the adult author was nonplused by his father's puzzled reaction to a life devoted to literature and political action. Yet, when he eventually wrote his brief autobiography in 1975, he recognized that there was more to the man than met his child's eye. In *Forbidden Territory* he describes the following scene:

> On another day, I suddenly entered my room and found him sitting on my bed, crying, with my mother's photograph in his hand. Ashamed at discovering something I did not wish to see, I quickly tiptoed out, without uttering a word. Today, this lack of filial pity and understanding of course seems shocking to me. (59)

The silence of the child is not overcome by the adult, because Goytisolo's father is dead when he writes these conciliatory words, but the harshness and self-centeredness of the child are unflinchingly observed. The emotion emerges years later, not only in the compassion for the desolate widower, but as a shocked disgust over his own lack of love and understanding. A similar delayed understanding and pain occur while he is viewing, in Paris twenty or more years after the event, newsreels of the air raid that killed his mother. The camera pans the faces of the dead, and Goytisolo is deeply shaken by the possibility that he might see his mother among the victims and the full horror of the situation will be exposed on screen. These two images—his father contemplating his

4

mother's photograph and Juan expecting his mother's image to appear—reveal the pain of a definitive absence. In these two scenes an image bridges the gap between a misunderstood situation and a subsequent understanding. The fullness of life is recovered only in recollection when, poignantly, in most instances it is too late to make amends.

Goytisolo's devotion to his father is manifest in his willingness to maintain for him, and for him alone, the dissimulation in political and sexual matters he had long ago dropped with others, a pretense he had come to abhor as the greatest and most abominable perversion. Only for his father does he seem not to evolve into complete agnosticism; only for him does he not profess Marxist sympathies or live openly as a homosexual. The section of *Forbidden Territory* where he reflects on this behavior is worth quoting in full:

> The impossibility of making him accept the true nature of my life doomed from the outset any pretense of dialogue. Our short, infrequent encounters in his last years teetered along under the pious cover of deceit. As we could not discuss crucial matters, our conversation was reduced to a string of commonplaces. Any revelation of my religious agnosticism, Marxist ideas, sexual behavior would have been an unbearable blow to him. It would have been gratuitously cruel to lead the conversation around to any of these topics. Condemned to dissimulation, I remained emotionally distanced from him, not worrying too much about his sad, frustrated life, mentally prepared for the time when he would disappear completely. (82–83)

Whether his father was also pretending not to know—he hardly could have remained completely uninformed of his son's preferences—we will never know. What matters is that this fundamental relationship with his father is described as a conflict that remains unresolvable yet tempered by affection. Goytisolo only acknowledged this affection years later, after a drug-induced dream in which he had a vision of his father, who had died in August 1964, when he experienced "an outburst of unsuspected tenderness for him" (83). Much of Goytisolo's writing is harsh, conflictive, and subversive, but this unsuspected and tender love is an underlying force in his creation.

The most important change Goytisolo hid from his father was his growing awareness of his homosexuality. Aside from the scorn that coming-out could bring at that time in Spain, and reaction could be vicious, Goytisolo had to deal with the repressed memory of an event that reverberates throughout his writings. When he was ten or eleven years old, as he describes in detail in *Forbidden Territory*, his maternal grandfather, who at the time lived with the family, repeatedly came to his bed during the night and molested him, while Juan pretended to sleep, embarrassed and perplexed. Eventually, Juan confided in his elder brother, José Agustín, who in turn revealed the nocturnal visits to his father. The grandfather and grandmother were expelled from their room and had to search for lodging elsewhere. In this sequence of events, the child experienced a loss of innocence and a pervasive sense of guilt that heralded for him a new period in relation to sexuality. The revelation that his grandfather had earlier lost his job because of his pedophilia, and the older man's subsequent humiliation, meekly accepted in front of his family and society, outraged Goytisolo, but not for the reason one might assume. Eventually, he took his grandfather's side, these nights becoming not a shameful memory but a secret initiation to the redeeming value of what may at first appear beyond the pale and unsalvageable.

Outside of the immediate family, there were three monumental institutions with which Goytisolo had to deal: school, church, and state. In Barcelona, after returning from the long break in his formal education brought about by the civil war, he started his schooling in a Jesuit school in 1939 but transferred with his other brothers in 1943 to another religious school, run by the Brothers of the Christian Doctrine. In 1948 he entered the University of Barcelona, beginning his studies in the faculties of law and literature with exemplary dedication, until in his second year, disillusioned with his professors and the prospects of a career in the foreign service, he began gradually to abandon his studies for a life dedicated to writing.

What we know from this period comes mainly from Juan Goytisolo himself, plus what can be gleaned in the autobiographical writings of his brother Luis, both in the latter's novel *Recuento* (1975, Recount) and in his partly autobiographical *Estatua con palomas* (1992, Statue with Pigeons). Juan, like most autobiographers, discounts the contribution of his formal education to the construction of his chosen self. The Jesuits are presented as masters of a rhetoric of fear and rigid discipline, much like those evoked by James Joyce in *A Portrait of the Artist as a Young Man*. The Brothers of the Christian Doctrine lack intellectual depth and latch on to shallow condemnations of Rousseau and Nietzsche. Bluntly, Goytisolo asserts: "Nothing that was said or happened in the classrooms influenced my life directly or indirectly" (*Forbidden Territory* 101). That statement is only partially true. The lack of intellectual challenge and the inadequate fit between formal education and vital experience made of him an outsider and autodidact with consequences that reverberate later in how the novelist conceives of his main characters, for whom isolation from institutions is a necessary precaution and individual effort the only possible successful action. Goytisolo, forced to find on his own a literature that would speak to his concerns, turned first to French and American literature—Proust, Gide, Malraux, Dos Passos, and Faulkner, among others—and only much later, when he was twenty-six years old and living in France, did he discover with the fervor of a convert, in an experience he compares to Paul's flash of revelation on his way to Damascus, *Don Quixote* and the writers of the Spanish Golden Age. He went on to read the Hispanist Américo Castro, who demonstrates conclusively the importance in Spanish history of contributions by Jews and Moors, who were expelled or forced to go underground during the Golden Age. Thus another revelation occurred: the Spain Goytisolo had rejected was a sham under which lay the body of the true nation, a nation to whose revival he would contribute and which he would bring to the attention of his compatriots and the world at large.

Those wasted hours in school provided another important and unavoidable lesson: the rhetoric of religion. In *Reivindicación del conde don Julián* (1970, *Count Julian*) and in *Juan sin tierra* (1975, *Juan the Landless*), he pokes fun at the ideal of perfection that sees sanctity in the denial of the body and such natural functions as sex and excretion. The language of the pulpit flows abundantly and with familiarity in these novels, with only the slightest of variations, in contexts that serve to warp sermons into ferocious satire. In his brief autobiographical sketch of 1975, he provides a compendium of how his nascent sexuality was permeated by remorse and religion: "Masturbaciones. Crisis de

7

arrepentimiento. Recaídas. Golpes de pecho. Propósitos de enmienda. Confesiones. Nuevos pecados" (13; Masturbations. Penitent crises. Repentance crises. New falls. Chest beating. Resolutions. Confessions. New sins). This cycle of pleasure, agony, remembrance, confession, and renewed pleasure, where someone else's ear and hand provide relief and absolution, is similar to his later activity of writing—also a frenzy of pleasure (writing) and agonized remembering—which he frequently equates with masturbation. He asks himself explicitly in *Forbidden Territory* if autobiography is not a secular substitute for the sacrament of confession (40). The importance of this similarity is that an activity that might appear to be an isolated act ends up requiring an interlocutor who functions much like a judge and a priest. If Goytisolo does not pander to his readers, but at times seems to turn against them aggressively, this is partly because the role the reader occupies is frequently that of the priest hearing a confession, and the priest is merely an unworthy representative of a higher power who knows all.

The intimate dialogue between the sacrament of confession and writing goes even deeper. Goytisolo tells us in *Forbidden Territory* that the idea of sin tortured him for several years (101), while in the autobiography of 1975 he dates his first religious doubts to 1947, when he was sixteen years old. At first blush he seems to have moved away from the Catholic church and reached a state where, at least in his sexual conduct, he was free from all guilt, because the conviction that, as he puts it, sex was natural and penicillin would cure any venereal illness "rid me entirely of guilt" (*Forbidden Territory* 103). But as will become evident in discussing his novels, when he moved away from the Catholicism of his childhood he retained the demanding goal of striving to live a virtuous life, even if understood in a radical way. Goytisolo's unremitting quest for sincerity, his continuing exploration of his thoughts and feelings, his solidarity with the despised and the marginal, his refusal to become a well-paid blip in the world of mass communications, his austere and almost monastic style of living—in short, his moral stance—all speak to the fact that Goytisolo may be, after all, one of the best students the Jesuits of Sarriá and the Brothers of the Christian Doctrine ever had.

It is not without significance that the greatest role model in Goytisolo's life has been the French writer Jean Genet, whom Sartre called most adequately, in the title of his study dedicated to this author, Saint Genet. Also, Goytisolo's deep-seated and increasing anxiety about death reveals a longing for transcendence, though a transcendence that does not require the intervention of any god. This sentiment is one of many in which Goytisolo's view resembles that of the philosopher and novelist Miguel de Unamuno (1864–1936), an author Goytisolo read avidly in his youth. In Goytisolo's recent novels, *Las virtudes del pájaro solitario* (1988, *The Virtues of the Solitary Bird*) and *La cuarentena* (1991, *Quarantine*), this yearning has found a kindred voice in the mystics of Islam and in Saint John of the Cross (1542–1591), another passionate pursuer of the truth who, like Goytisolo today, seemed to many in the established order of his time too passionate and too extreme.

After being graduated from the ranks of the Jesuits and the Brothers, Goytisolo moved on to the university, where he found his professors' lectures uninspiring. After five years of increasingly desultory studies, Goytisolo abandoned the pursuit of a law degree, but it was during this period that he met friends who expanded his horizons in politics, litera-ture, and sexual practices. He became aware, through voracious reading, feverish conversation, and repeated visits to the seediest parts of Barcelona, of a different world where poverty was injustice, crime an art, and sex an unashamed industry. He encountered, in his nightlife ex-peditions, people and situations that Dostoevski, Marx, Gide, and Sartre had prepared him to understand. The Other and the Forbidden emerged then as privileged categories encompassing all that is valuable and at-tractive for Goytisolo and his literary alteregos.

His brother Luis became a member of the Communist party and was imprisoned in 1960 for a brief period in Carabanchel prison. In Luis's opinion, Juan was little more than a dandy and a pretentious beginner among the literati. Juan did, however, attempt to learn more about Marx-ism, only to feel repelled by the authoritarian structure of the Commu-nist party and its uninspiring literature. Luis was to give, in *Recuento*, a detailed and masterful account of the clandestine, but mostly futile, ac-tivities of university students during the 1950s and of the ponderous speeches of Escala, one of their revered leaders. More iconoclastic is Juan Marsé, who, in *Ultimas tardes con Teresa* (1966, *Last Evenings with Teresa*), shows the illusory nature of most attempts of well-off university students to express their solidarity with the poor and marginal and the hopelessness of attempting to close the gap of social class and wealth with language and sex. Goytisolo's first published novel, *Juegos de manos* (1954, *The Young Assassins*) describes the dangerous and mostly sterile search for meaningful social action of a group of well-to-do youngsters who wear their existential angst on their sleeves. His flirtation with Marxism in subsequent years left an imprint in Fiestas, a 1958 novel about the poor of Barcelona, and led Juan to many activities as a sympathizer, which he describes at length in the second part of his autobiography, *En los reinos de taifa* (1986, *Realms of Strife*). Ultimately the transformation of Spain from dictatorship to democracy did not come as a result of the clandestine activities of young intellectuals, but through the impact of tourism, capitalism, and modern communications. Goytisolo, fortunately, was not only a political activist, but was embarked in a deeper and longer-range personal liberation that involved geography, passion, and writing.

As a child with an active imagination, Juan was enthralled with geography and maps, a tendency stimulated in his case by his uncle Leopoldo, who never left Barcelona but was a devoted imaginary traveler. During the summers the Goytisolo family spent in their house at Torrentbó, the adolescent Juan chatted with Leopoldo about America, Africa, and India, consulting books and maps and reveling in the promise of a different and exotic existence. Juan came to believe that there was a place where happiness and truth were more easily attainable, a belief that would run through his writings and idealize a place successively located in the red-light district of Barcelona, in Paris, and in Marrakesh. As will be detailed in later chapters, Juan aligns himself in his novels and essays with distinguished travelers of the past, such as Lawrence of Arabia and Sir Richard Burton. Contrary to the conservative and bourgeois principle that life as it currently is represents the highest accomplishment of historical evolution, Juan found in his maps and imaginary travels the inspiration to affirm otherwise: there could be, there was, a different and better life, elsewhere, away from the safety of his Barcelona home.

A first trip to Paris in 1953 seemed to confirm this childhood dreams. He reveled there in the abundance of books, films, theater, and music.

He saw in cafés the exiles from the Spanish civil war, still discussing over coffee military campaigns long ago lost in the field but won many times since, thanks to an ingenious new maneuver that could have saved the day. After his return to Barcelona, where he wrote *Duelo en el paraíso* (*Children of Chaos*) in 1954 (published in 1955), he remained interested in French literature and French music. Barcelona had become for him only a transient home, and, instead of settling down, Juan gave himself over to a nomadic quest of renovation through uprooting. He returned briefly to Paris in 1955 and then traveled to Spain for six months for his military service. Back in France, he moved into an apartment in the rue Poissonnière with Monique Lange, a writer and an editor in the transla-tion department of the Gallimard publishing house. In later years he trav-eled to the Soviet Union, Cuba, Canada, the United States, and through northern Africa, until he discovered Marrakesh, which became his sec-ond home. Goytisolo was not attracted by the glitter of cities or tourist shrines. He celebrated snatches of immigrant diversity, the bustle of anonymous streets, the pandemonium of the marketplace.

At the time of his geographical discoveries, Goytisolo was engaged in a corresponding exploration of the self. In the 1960s, Goytisolo be-came acutely aware that the family name was not only an arbitrary tag, but also an indication that he had come into existence as a player with an assigned role. He had already shrugged off or modified some family, religious, and patriotic expectations. Sexual identity, however, proved more complex. In Spanish society of the Franco period, deeply marked by the military and the church, sex, except as a flirtation of allusive im-ages or muffled titillation, was expunged from films, novels, radio, and any other form of official public speech that could fall into the hands of the innocent and unsuspecting. Whatever images remained concerned heterosexual sex. Writers such as the Spanish poets Federico García Lorca (1898–1936) and Luis Cernuda (1902–1963), the Irish Oscar Wilde (1854–1900), and the French Nobel Prize winner for literature in 1947, André Gide (1869–1951), represented troubling exceptions, their works admired but their private lives reviled. As in most countries of the world at a time before the Stonewall Riots of June 1969 in New York City, in which groups of gay men and women resisted police harassment outside a homosexual bar, and the start of gay and lesbian liberation movements which have flourished in the last three decades, all official forms of communication proclaimed that a man who loved another man was engaged in a shameful and disruptive act. Goytisolo tells in his autobiography how he did not experience the expected adolescent interest in the opposite sex, a difference from his friends that left him disoriented and perplexed.[1] He certainly had no conscious desire to emulate the humiliating behavior of his maternal grandfather or to run against the prevailing wisdom among most of his friends, who professed a virulent abomination of gays. A series of anecdotes told in *Forbidden Territory* and in *Realms of Strife* points to an evolution closely examined in his literature.

In most autobiographies—partly because they are written by people who consider writing important enough to transform their own lives into a book—a deciding event is the encounter with a text that brings news of a different and more desirable life. Saint Augustine is exhorted by a child's voice he happens to hear while sitting in his garden to lift a book and read, occasioning his memorable conversion when he encounters Paul's words and their call to a higher life. Saint Teresa affirms the truth of her experiences against the barrage of male authority after reading Francisco de Osuna's manual of meditation, *Tercer abecedario espiritual.* Diego de Torres Villarroel, an eighteenth-century professor at the University of Salamanca and the author of an excellent autobiography that Goytisolo knew well, breaks off his picaresque life and heads into the venerable classrooms of his native town after reading some scientific books, especially one by the German mathematician Christophorus Clavius (1537–1612), left over from the sale of his father's bookstore. Blanco White, later in that century, in his autobiography recognizes the vigor of critical thought after riffling through the volumes of the complete works of the eighteenth-century Spanish essayist Feijoo (1676–1764).

Goytisolo's case is more oblique. In *Forbidden Territory*, he is alarmed when he hears a book salesman spread a rumor that he is homosexual because, among the books he had ordered, were works by Gide and Wilde. Outraged, Goytisolo convinces a friend to invite the rumormonger to his house and confront him while Goytisolo listens, hidden behind a half-open door. The salesman has no proof but sticks to his opinion, invoking the names of several of Goytisolo's friends who are both admirers of Gide and known homosexuals. This is a significant scene in which the truth is spoken but not recognized by the conscious mind. The bookseller's insight comes from Goytisolo's choice of readings, a method of attribution that Goytisolo himself will strongly endorse in his later literature. Though the salesman is dismissed parenthetically as a scion "from a well-off family who would be arrested months later for his involvement in an armed robbery" (145), peddling his books from door to door until betting his future on an instant of violent crime, as if he had walked into a novel written by Juan Marsé, he presents an interesting contrast with the other member of a "well-off family," Juan Goytisolo, overhearing from his hiding place this ultimately correct diagnosis of his sexual orientation. How much Juan depended then on the good opinion of others, an aspect of the youthful writer's character repeatedly stressed by his brother Luis in his own memoirs, can be gleaned from how Juan remembers that it was not the possibility of being homosexual that distressed him, but that others could include him in that despised and reportedly degraded group. A further incident, a drunken embrace with a Colombian friend in Madrid, increases his disquiet and his efforts to demonstrate his manliness to his friends by cavorting with prostitutes.

In 1955 Goytisolo, during a stay in Paris, met two people who significantly affected his life, Monique Lange and Jean Genet.[2] With Lange, Goytisolo discovered the pleasures of heterosexual love and of a longlasting relationship. In chapter five of *Realms of Strife*, he evokes her movingly as an enlightened, intelligent, and supportive companion. Working with her at Gallimard, Goytisolo met many of the famous intellectuals of Paris, among them Albert Camus, Marguerite Duras, and Simone de Beauvoir. Monique and Juan shared leftist politics and a fascination for the unusual, including an affection for transvestites and gay bars. Goytisolo enjoyed stepping into the role of a father to Monique's daughter from her recently ended marriage but refused to be called "father," a designation that carried for him the baggage of too many conflictive emotions. Still, the relationship with Monique soured in the early 1960s when Juan became jealous and possessive while at the same time immersed in his own homoerotic adventures. He was especially attracted by men who were from a lower class, foreign, and lacked any other sophistication than a vigorous nature. Not coincidentally, during this period in which his chosen truth about his self was beginning to emerge and relations with Monique were stranded in duplicity, he wrote the novel that opens the period of maturity in his writing, *Señas de identidad* (*Marks of Identity*), published in 1966, a novel about a Spanish intellectual who returns from France to film a documentary and discovers that not only has Spain hidden her past but he, the denouncer and revealer, has repressed and avoided his own truth.

In 1965 he was invited to visit the Soviet Union and decided that the time was ripe to confess his homosexual affairs to Monique, figuring that because they would be separated for at least a week, this would give her time to digest the news. What he had been unable to say to her face to face, even with her gentle and seemingly knowing prodding, was at last written down in a letter. This letter is transcribed, with a few deletions, in *Realms of Strife*. It is the transcript of a painful personal circumstance, but it is also a text sent from one writer to another, and it has been transformed into literature by its inscription in the autobiography. As such, it can be studied as a masterpiece of rhetoric—understood as the knowledgeable use of strategies of persuasion—and a memorable piece of writing. It also places the reader behind the half-open door of the page, looking over Goytisolo's shoulders as he makes this most painful and liberating confession. The writer in turn knows that his public extends beyond Monique, that first some intimate friends will pour over these pages, then casual readers and literary critics. But he may not have anticipated in 1965 that his letter would be included twenty-one years later among the pages of the wiser and elder Goytisolo's autobiography. In this new context, the younger Juan's text becomes slick, and denying his lover the right to rebuttal seems cruel.

The letter starts by explaining his need to reveal an important matter that he does not dare trust to the vagaries of a conversation. He immediately stresses that he is sure of her love, which he returns even more than in earlier years, except physically, because only men attract him. The next paragraph claims that Monique had fascinated him precisely because of her "masculinity," and that therefore for years his homosexual tendencies were assuaged. Things had begun to deteriorate, he claims, when her flirting with other men had reduced him to occasional impotence and depression. For his despair he could only find refuge in homosexual life. In the next paragraph, though, he recovers his fairness and shifts his argument away from burdening Monique with the responsibility of wrecking their relationship. For a year now, he acknowledges, he has had sexual encounters with Arabs, and he has come to the conclusion that he is definitely homosexual. The revelation of this truth to Monique was postponed because he had not wanted to shatter the supportive atmosphere he wished to create for her. She had left Gallimard in 1964, depressed by her mother's death, and retired to Saint-Tropez, with Juan and her daughter, Carole, to write. There is also Carole to think about, to whom the news of Juan's homosexuality could cause a "damaging impact" (205). He throws himself on Monique's mercy, laying the final decision on her lap: "I am thirty-four, I love you, and I love Carole, I cannot live without you, I feel a boundless affection for you. What should I do? The void that life alone would be terrifies me, but I will accept it if that is what you decide" (205). The letter ends with new professions of love, implying that he does not want to break their relationship, only to modify it and include a space for his homosexual attachments.

When Monique joined Goytisolo in Moscow a week later, she had with her a response, also in the form of a letter, which is not included in his autobiography. An old and strong affection, generosity, and the openness of courageous people immersed in the daring spirit of the 1960s prevailed. The example of Simone de Beauvoir and Jean-Paul Sartre, at the time the best-known case of leading intellectuals with an open and independent relationship as lovers—the more sordid details had not yet emerged—was available to them as an encouraging model, as well as the unconventional and profound wisdom of their good friend Jean Genet, who could find a sort of happiness in any relation and situation. Juan and Monique were married 17 August 1978 in Paris.

The other fateful encounter of 1955 was with Jean Genet, who had been born in 1910 and was twenty-one years Goytisolo's elder. Genet did not come from a privileged background: his mother was probably a prostitute who abandoned him to an orphanage, and he never knew who his father was. He was educated in the countryside in central France under the care of a peasant family, apparently enjoying a happy childhood until he was ten years old. Then, branded as a thief, he spent most of his adolescence in a reformatory. From the time of his release, he lived a vagrant life as a petty thief, visiting, among other countries, Spain. In his novels he describes crime, treason, and degradation as forms of discipline and virtue. Genet can be convincing because he rescues all aspects of human life with the eyes of a mystic and the language of a poet. As the saints of old could face leprosy with compassion, Genet extols manifestations of life that are marginalized by society as deviant or morally repugnant. He makes the portraits of his homosexual lovers glow with reverence, beauty, and love, even redeeming in this all-encompassing vision their roles as pimps, drugpushers, thieves, brutal policemen, or professional beggars. His extraordinary talent as a writer, the classical elegance of his style, was present from the time of his first book, written in prison, *Our Lady of the Flowers* (1943), and would gain him the attention and respect of numerous French intellectuals, among them Sartre and the poet and playwright Jean Cocteau (1889–1963), who organized a successful campaign to have Genet released from prison.

In 1949 Genet published *The Thief's Journal,* an autobiographical account in which he describes in detail, but with no shame or self-compassion, a life well beyond the bounds of acceptability for a French intellectual. A long section concerns his experiences in Barcelona and southern Spain, describing as an insider the world of the lower classes which Goytisolo would find attractive in his younger years. Genet's audacity and lack of concern for the applause of the bourgeoisie served as a model for Goytisolo, who recounts in two different instances in his own autobiographical work his important first encounter with Genet at Monique's apartment. In the recounting of events of that evening, Genet turns abruptly to him and asks him if he is homosexual. Goytisolo mumbles an embarrassed reply, to the effect that he has had homosexual experiences. Genet chides him for his tepid and uncommitted remark and proceeds to ignore Goytisolo the rest of the evening. Genet had taught him the important lesson he needed to learn: there was much to see and conquer in his own mind, where the opinion of others still lurked and controlled his actions, before he could criticize society's hypocrisy. For Goytisolo, it was incredibly difficult to become vulnerable, open, accepting of one's faults, truly and deeply free from external and internal authorities. They would eventually become good friends, and, more important, Goytisolo, in Genet, had found a model for his own path.

History and Language

Goytisolo's life has occupied us up until now because his two volumes of autobiography and the extensive autobiographical content of many of his novels show that these events and memories are for him the basic materials of his writing. His life, as remembered in his books, is a succession of stages of innocence that crumble under the revelation of a new truth, leading to another stage that in turn is brittle and transient. His life gets explained by the literature, but in a varied series of replaceable modes—existential, sociological, semiotic, poststructuralist, postmodern—that readers should know offer no definitive description, even if the narrator appears to have reached ultimate illumination each time. It is conceivable that Goytisolo could write, several decades in the future, a very different autobiography. Resembling the heroes of Kierkegaard and Nietzsche, he makes a virtue of an inconsistency that is necessary to approach the shifting truths of life. He is aware that all human life, when it is remembered, is a stream of images and memories structured as a narrative. Otherwise, it would be an infinite sequence of unconnected instants.

In his autobiographical volumes, Goytisolo frequently reflects on— many times in a different voice marked by italic type, as in a dramatic aside—how he is constructing a written life, perhaps betraying the younger Goytisolo who lived what is now only remembered experiences. But even at the time of writing, many of those events were perceived through the mesh of ideals and projects deeply marked by his readings. Sartre, in his autobiography *The Words* (1963), recalls the impact a book called *The Childhood of Famous Men* had on him as a child. Future greatness could be announced in apparently trivial responses or actions. Cervantes, Raphael, Molière, and Rousseau were all once children, and a perceptive biographer can always glean in the record the prefigurement of greatness. Sartre began to see himself through the eyes of the future and to seed intentionally moments that could satisfy posterity—shifting through his conversations of the day to find the memorable nugget, or sitting at his desk without a light after darkness fell to be able to utter "I could write even in the dark" (205).

While he remembers this posing with ironic affection, noting that he has became his own obituary, it is nevertheless a fact that this snippet of his childhood is recalled, analyzed, and monumentalized in writing for the instruction of future children who wish to emulate him. Saint Augustine stealing pears, Saint Teresa escaping from home with her brother Rodrigo to convert the infidels, Rousseau unjustly accused of breaking a comb, the English historian Edward Gibbon's (1737–1794) early and invincible love of reading that he "would not exchange for all the treasures of India" (*Memoirs* 67)—these are some of the instances autobiographers chew over because they seem to contain important clues to their personalities. Here they find the radiance of a continued self: the persistence of original sin and the capacity to overcome it in Augustine, the release of missionary zeal normally restrained by society in Teresa, the love of justice in an unfair society in Rousseau, and the historian's devotion to knowledge in Gibbon.

But in the process of separating the wheat from the chaff remains the question of how to deal with the embarrassing elements of one's own past. Augustine's willingness to sacrifice his lover to advance his career through an advantageous marriage, Teresa's frivolous and passionate reading of novels of chivalry, Rousseau's convenient conversion to Catholicism and the methodical forwarding of all his children to an orphanage, Gibbon's breaking his engagement to a Swiss woman when recalled to England by a distressed father who threatened to disinherit him—all these are shameful memories. They tarnish the self-image and are dislocating and alienating. To the places in the past that could be called the home of the present self—of the one who writes the autobiography—they add another territory where an alternative self could have been grounded. That other self is not recognized under the sign of sameness but of difference, as an alien incarnation. In the case of Goytisolo, he rejects as autobiographer any similarity with the diligent child who struggled to please his elders, with the dandy socialite of adolescence, with the first-year university student who lobbied his professors for higher grades, and with the combative believer in the social function of literature. He often returns to images of demonic possession and alludes to

18

Robert Louis Stevenson's 1886 story "The Strange Case of Dr. Jekyll and Mr. Hyde" to show the conflictive, even destructive interdependence between disparate aspects of his personality. This intruding Other can be the accomplished dandy seen from the vantage point of later years, or the rebellious homosexual seen through the eyes of the younger person.

The dangers of this delimitation of two selves and the difficulty of narrating their history are clear to Goytisolo, who writes in one of the meditative sections marked off in the italics of *Forbidden Territory*:

> *Awareness of the dangers and snares of the enterprise: futile attempt to erect a bridge over the discontinuity of your biography, to grant coherence after the event to a mere accumulation of ruins: looking for the underground channel that nourishes the chronological succession of events in some way without being sure whether it is an archeologist's dig or a dazzling work of engineering. . . .* (164)

The gap or "discontinuity" emerges only when life is written down. Because of similar biographical situations, Robert Louis Stevenson (1850–1894) was a kindred spirit for Goytisolo: the son of a prosperous engineer, Stevenson received a strict religious education and was expected to follow in his father's footsteps. Instead, he studied law at Edinburgh University, became an agnostic bohemian, started to write, and left for France, America, and the South Pacific, where he settled in Samoa for the last years of his life. What "The Strange Case of Dr. Jekyll and Mr. Hyde" tells us is that two sides of a personality can only be separated temporarily and at great risk by a chemical compound—or by writing. To return to previous examples, Augustine's expediency and ambition provide the impulse for his routing of Manichaeans and pagans in northern Africa; Teresa's early readings may have left her with traces of what became the metaphors of love she applied later to express her mystical experiences; Gibbon's pusillanimity forced him into a retiring life with a modest income, providing him the perfect conditions for writing his history of *The Decline and Fall of the Roman Empire*; Rousseau's egoism, exhibitionism, and self-serving paranoia took autobiography to a level of self-scrutiny never reached before. Similarly, the younger

Goytisolo returns, side by side with the heterodox older self, obsessed with telling the truth, doing the right thing, working diligently, and establishing a record of his accomplishments. Goytisolo expresses throughout his autobiography an ambition to be rid of the past, to betray previously held values, and to erase the signs of identity that come with family, religion, country, gender, and language. Autobiography allows him to create this desired distance with the past, but only at the price of recreating it. While Goytisolo as the narrator of his life attains a significant degree of freedom, as an author he has become even more deeply entangled, by remembering it so effectively, with a past that sticks fast to his signature.

Another difficulty in his desire for cancellation and erasure is that his path of liberation is the path of language, not of silence, as it is of remembering and not forgetting. Growing up in a Castilian-speaking household in Barcelona, he was handed down a wounded and dispirited language. He was also ignorant of the depth of Catalan culture, whose expression had been reduced by Franco's dictatorship to the whispers of the familial and the shadows of the library. As mentioned before, for many of his formative years, Goytisolo read mostly in French and only later discovered the Spanish Golden Age. The immediate consequence is that his early novels suffer from a stilted language and unintended roughness of style. Their power lies more in the idea than in the flow of a particular paragraph. In 1977, for the first volume of a projected publication of his complete works, which included novels originally published between 1954 and 1958, Goytisolo introduced innumerable changes, without warning readers that they were confronted with carefully revised versions.

In Spain such a renewal was necessary not only for Goytisolo but for all Spanish novelists. The literature of the 1940s, immediately after the civil war, offers three or four memorable novels and many others that are discreetly accomplished, yet much of it reads like epigonal continuations of a sordid form of naturalism with a dash of borrowed existentialism. Camilo José Cela's *La familia de Pascual Duarte* (1942, *The Family of Pascual Duarte*), Torrente Ballester's *Javier Mariño* (1943), and Carmen Laforet's *Nada* (1945, *Nada*), introduce unforgettable characters and are in some degree experimental. The disorienting chronology and proliferation of points of view in *Pascual Duarte* and the essay-istic forays of *Javier Mariño* were daring for their time. *Nada*, the story of an adolescent who arrives in Barcelona to study at the university, has a sharp phantasmagoric edge and blends in elements of romance and fairy tales in a way that much later would be considered fashionably postmodern. But for Goytisolo and other writers close to him—Ana María Matute, Carmen Martín Gaite, Rafael Sánchez Ferlosio, Ignacio Aldecoa—these earlier stories of a rural assassin, a violent Falangist, and a dysfunctional family seemed provincial and less skillful than they actually were. Furthermore, not only was Castilian the language of a unity imposed by Madrid, but it was also the language of a powerful and effective publicity machine funded by the state and underpinned by cen-sorship, as will be explained in the next chapter. The central government's constant need to flex its muscles suffocated writers by means of a pre-scribed morality and a restricted vocabulary. Since an important part of the Spanish cultural tradition was actively ignored—the Arab inherit-ance, the Catalan and Basque nationalities, Republican values—words such as *motherland, empire, greatness, originality,* and *seriousness* car-ried with them the echoes of conservative and often reactionary reso-nances. For Goytisolo and many others, then, Castilian was a language in need of liberation.

To understand Goytisolo, therefore, it helps to see his life—his ef-forts to become independent from his family, to outgrow his education, to generate his own choices, and to find values he can believe in, as well as his incessant search for new forms of writing—not as a narcissistic quest, but as representative of a country emerging from an amnesiac nightmare. This is not to say that Goytisolo has ever wanted to be a leader in any battle other than in writing better novels. He firmly states that he does not wish to be seen as an exile or a gay liberator. He carries no party's card. And his value as a writer far transcends his conscious and unconscious testimonial of a period in Spain's history. But if one takes into account that his literature is deeply involved in a spirited dia-logue, at times an acrimonious controversy, with the circumstances of his life, with Spain's contemporary history, and with the conditions of Spanish language, his accomplishments emerge with greater clarity in all their admirable power.

Notes

1. His perplexity was probably in part due to the fact that his sexuality does not seem to fall into a neat category—heterosexual or homosexual—but corresponds more to what Weinberg, Williams, and Pryor describe in *Dual Attraction: Understanding Bisexuality*. Unfortunately, this book and its ideas were unavailable to Goytisolo, since *Dual Attraction* appeared in 1994 and is presented by the authors as a groundbreaking study of sexual practices not well understood before.

2. To keep this chapter within reasonable boundaries, I have chosen in the following pages to select only a few of the most important encounters with persons and books in Goytisolo's intellectual life. In a different version of these pages one could highlight the importance, for example, of Georges Bataille (1897–1962), Américo Castro (1885–1972), or the Marquis de Sade (1740–1814).

CHAPTER TWO

How to Read Goytisolo

Writing as Political Activity during the Franco Era (1939–1975)

When Juan Goytisolo was starting his career in the 1950's, the most significant literary prize in Spain was the annual Nadal award. The writer was handsomely rewarded, the text speedily published and expertly distributed. In 1954 Goytisolo entered in the competition the manuscript of *Juegos de manos* (*The Young Assassins*), which was a finalist but lost to a novel by Luisa Forellad, *Siempre en capilla* (Always in the Death House). She recounts the adventures in nineteenth-century England of three medical doctors who fight a diphtheria epidemic with a combination of hygiene, scientific progress, and religious faith. This topic was a safe one, conveniently uplifting and far-removed from the political and economic tensions at home. On the contrary, Goytisolo's novel deals with rebellious youths and murder. The editors promptly informed him, as he recollects in *Forbidden Territory*, that they were interested in his manuscript but found its publication improbable, given the restrictions of censorship.

More than a decade after the Spanish civil war ended in 1939 with the victory of the conservative alliance backing Gen. Francisco Franco, the government tightly controlled travel abroad and the circulation of potentially subversive ideas. Camilo José Cela, whose immensely successful novel *The Family of Pascual Duarte* had been briefly banned in 1943, found it advisable in 1951 to publish his scathing, somber, and technically brilliant *La colmena* (*The Beehive*) in faraway Buenos Aires. In spite of being at the time Spain's best-known young novelist, Cela was expelled from the journalists' union. Gonzalo Torrente Ballester's career was derailed when his *Javier Mariño* was considered too vehement and extremist and was banned in 1943, the year of its publication. Not until the 1960s, after working most of his life as a high school teacher, would Torrente Ballester finally be recognized as one of Spain's master novelists.

To understand the difficulties writers in the 1940s experienced with censorship we can take as an illustrative case the fate of García Serrano's *La fiel infantería* (The Faithful Infantry). Rafael García Serrano fought in the civil war on the Nationalist side—against the republic and on the side of the insurgent Franco—and was a devoted believer of the ideas of the Falange, a political movement whose charismatic leader, José Antonio Primo de Rivera (1903–1936), was executed by the Republicans at the outset of the war.[1] García Serrano was discharged from active duty in order to get treatment for his tuberculosis, a sickness that constituted a terrible epidemic in a country where the destruction of major cities, roads, and industries and the drop in agricultural production had brought hunger, corruption, and misery. From 1939 to 1941 he wrote *La fiel infantería*. This portrait of military life in the combat zone is written with a wry and scathing pen and a penchant for brutal details and vulgar expressions.

In 1943 the official governmental press, the Editora Nacional, published *La fiel infantería*, which was received with divided opinions by the readers: some found it a realistic portrait of men at war, while others considered it an insult. Especially offensive was that the novels showed defenders of Catholicism against anarchism and Marxism as blasphemous and obsessed with sex. Late in December of 1943 the novel received the National Prize for literature as the best novel of the year. In January 1944 the archbishop of Toledo published an extended condemnation of the novel. He gave the following reasons: it presents the sin of lust as necessary and inevitable among young people; it describes scenes in a cabaret and a whorehouse, uses swearwords, and includes unbelievers among the Nationalist soldiers. Soon after, the Catholic press attacked the book and the police removed all copies from bookstores. In 1945 the bishop sent García Serrano a copy of *La fiel infantería* with all its offensive words underlined in red, offering to authorize a new edition if they were removed. This extraordinary document, the text and its marginalia, was published in 1973 and shows the bishop objecting, for example, to the mention of the existence of obscene graffiti on a wall, a pagan peasant, a priest participating in looting, some adolescents reading pornographic novels, and the splendid legs of a woman dancer.

Goytisolo inherited a tradition of repression and accommodation in the publishing world. With a few cuts, *The Young Assassins* was published because the influential editor of Planeta, José Manuel Lara, recognized the talent of the young writer and saw him as a marketable commodity. Goytisolo's second novel, *Children of Chaos*, had among its characters soldiers in the civil war. The censors of this novel deleted all swearwords from the mouths of Nationalists but allowed some to be used by the Republicans. Goytisolo purged them all, leaving both sides' speeches equally refined and equally improbable in vocabulary.

This collaboration between censor and author in the deletion of offensive words was the price paid to reach his public but carried with it the seed of a corrosive yet easily acquired habit: self-censorship. Many authors encoded their works with symbols and dreamlike sequences to reach the conscience of the nation. Goytisolo, though, was alert to the insidious effect of silencing and disfiguring the truth. Eventually, he realized that authors who internalize censorship run the risk of producing tinted, deformed, and partial images.

Goytisolo's *El circo* (The Circus) was published in Spain in 1957, while two other novels found more hospitable presses in 1958: *Fiestas* (*Fiestas*) was published in Buenos Aires, and *La resaca* (The Undertow) in Paris. Two years later he published in Spain a travel book, *Campos de Níjar* (*The Countryside of Níjar*), which was translated the following year into Italian. A documentary film which complemented this last book, but which had not been made by Goytisolo, was being shown in Milan when a bomb exploded, and the film was stolen. The film resurfaced a few days later in Spain, where it was shown on national television in a greatly doctored version. Goytisolo appeared responsible for a documentary intended to denigrate Spain abroad, and therefore his reputation in Spain suffered a severe blow, bringing censorship to a devastating level. This was added to the fact that in 1960 the censors had denied authorization to publish *La isla* (*Island of Women*), which was instead issued the following year by a Mexican imprint of the Barcelona publishing house Seix Barral. The priest who read it for the first censorship report noted that the novel was a detailed account of eleven days spent in Torremolinos by a group of degenerates with no moral orientation. For him, the novel was nothing more than barbarous expressions and incessant fornication. A second priest and censor found it obscene, disrespectful of the victorious side of the civil war and of the church, and morbidly unprincipled.

These reports, reproduced as an appendix in Jesús Lázaro's book on Goytisolo, are not simply the adverse conditions which a writer confronted. The reports, plus the many paragraphs of the manuscript of *Island of Women* annotated by the censors as politically, ethically, or sexually unacceptable, show that writing in Spain had become for many novelists a contest with the censors. Writers transmuted novels into cryptograms and produced mutilated texts reveling in clever ambiguity but scarred and plagued with omissions and gaps. Goytisolo's *Marks of Identity* was published in Mexico in 1966, and not until 1975—the year of Franco's death—did he resume publishing novels in Spain with *Juan the Landless*.

Censorship also created a void in the reporting of social conditions in the country, since newspapers and the radio were tightly controlled by the restrictive laws regarding the press, promulgated on 22 April 1938 and not abrogated until 1966. Up until 1962 newspapers had to submit all copy to the censors, a procedure that continued to be necessary after that date for newspapers in Barcelona and Madrid. Herbert L. Matthews, a *New York Times* correspondent, in 1957 called the Spanish press "one of the greatest insults to the intelligence of the Western World" (101), but Henry F. Schulte, in *The Spanish Press, 1470–1966*, argues, taking a longer view, that press control under Franco "represented nothing new in Spain's history of government-press relations. The pendulum has merely swung to the extreme of controls in theory as well as practice" (242). While not new, Spanish censorship was drastic, and Schulte titles his chapter devoted to the Franco years "The Padlocked Mouth." He recounts that one journalist was denounced when he reported a lower than expected orange crop, while another was arrested and fined for publishing a story about a poliomyelitis epidemic. A third newsman was arrested for criticizing defects in a public housing project. Schulte further recalls that of the 110 daily newspapers in Spain, 38 were Falangist organs providing a party slant to the news. Filtered news from abroad occupied much space and was frequently read as encoded allusions to muffled national scandals or debates. International journals were closely scrutinized, and, during 1954 alone, twenty issues of the *New York Times* were banned from Spain.

Reporting about the literary scene was also severely curtailed, as can be gleaned from the following paragraph:

> At the beginning of 1956, the government closed down the literary reviews *Indice* and *Insula* because they had violated newsprint regulations. Prior to 1956, the two magazines had courted official disfavor by publishing, with laudatory comments, the work of exiled Spanish writers. In 1955, when philosopher José Ortega y Gasset died, the Ministry of Information issued an order outlining coverage of his death. "Each newspaper," the order said, "may publish up to three articles relative to the death of Ortega y Gasset: a biography and two commentaries. Every article on the writer's philosophy must underline his errors in religious matters. It is permissible to publish photographs of the mortuary on the front page, of the death mask or body of Ortega, but no photographs made during his lifetime." *Indice* and *Insula* exceeded their authorized number of pages in issues devoted to Ortega y Gasset and were closed. *Indice* reappeared at the end of 1956, *Insula* the following year. (Schulte 38)

Writers could not bear these controls with indifference. While much of what passed for journalism crossed the line into fantasy—reporting a never-never land of peace, prosperity, and happiness—novelists became the journalists of their country. Goytisolo and most of the best writers of his time found an inspiration in novels, films, and philosophy. American novels about the harsh life in the cities and the suffering of working people during the Depression, such as Dos Passos's *Manhattan Transfer* of 1925 and Steinbeck's *The Grapes of Wrath* of 1939, provided different examples of literary reporting.

Italian neorealist novels and especially movies, with their stark look and documentary style, were greatly admired in the early 1950s, since Spanish cinema also suffered from censorship. Dubbing, cutting, and banning took their toll on creative talent, in a struggle well documented by Virginia Higginbotham in *Spanish Film Under Franco*. Therefore, it was a memorable event when the Institute of Italian Culture held an Italian Film Week in Madrid in 1951. A selection of forbidden films of stunning quality dazzled the public, which contained many students from the National Film School. Among other films, they saw Antonioni's *Chronicle of Love* (1950), De Sica's *Bicycle Thief* (1948) and *Miracle in Milan* (1951), and Rossellini's *Open City* (1945) and *Paisá* (1946), movies that are still considered remarkable for their technical creativity and their wrenching compassion for underdogs.

In the realm of ideas, Jean-Paul Sartre (1905–1980), Albert Camus (1913–1960), Georg Lukács (1885–1971), and Antonio Gramsci (1891–1937) provided in different ways a philosophical framework for putting literature at the service of communicating the repressed ills of society. Sartre made of his insight on human freedom, the result of our conscience being a nonthing, a paradoxical obligation to make all choices social and to forgo the myth of an independent art for art's sake. His *What Is Literature?* was first published in French in 1948, the same year in which all his works were condemned by the Catholic church. It was published in a Spanish translation in Buenos Aires in 1950. This essay could not hope to be generally well received in Spain, where Sartre's works had been frequently and strongly attacked during the 1940s.[2] Yet Sartre's *engagement* or commitment soon became a household idea all over Europe. The same can be said of Camus's humanism, as represented in his editorials in the resistance newspaper *Combat* or in his 1945 *Letters to a German Friend.* Through the Marxist underground, Gramsci's *Letters from Prison*, first published in Italian in 1947, and Lukács's *Theory of the Novel*, a study the Hungarian philosopher published in 1920, were also available to stimulate the involvement of intellectuals in a process of social activism.

In 1956 and 1957 Goytisolo published a series of spirited essays which he collected in his book of 1959 *Problemas de la novela* (Problems of the Novel). In them he defends the objective stance of the narrator who allows his characters to express their views and communicate their lives. He sees literature as part of a social process of understanding those who are too poor, ignored, or oppressed to be able to speak for themselves. He extols the North American novelists, such as Hemingway, Faulkner, Caldwell, and Steinbeck, who stand aside to let their world be, without commentary from the author, yet is less enthusiastic about the

French new novelist Alain Robbe-Grillet's extreme objectivity denuded of social commentary. Goytisolo laments the lack of breadth of Spanish authors, who are mostly middle-class intellectuals, as opposed to their American counterparts who have had numerous jobs where they have gathered firsthand experience about the workingman's world. The tradition contemporary writers should follow, according to Goytisolo's argument in this book, is that initiated by the Spanish picaresque novel of the Golden Age, unflinchingly critical of the society it portrayed from the point of view of the lower classes. He celebrates the work of the Italian neorealists, especially Elio Vittorini (1908–1966), a novelist, essayist, and translator of North American books, who was imprisoned for one of his novels and agitated for a literature less involved with aesthetics than with politics. Goytisolo defends the recently published novels of Jesús Fernández Santos and Rafael Sánchez Ferlosio, *Los bravos* (1954, The Braves) and *El Jarama* (1956, *The One Day of the Week*), respectively, two novels that have since taken their place among the best of that decade but were received then with perplexity for their apparent documentary nature in describing a few days in a small town and a day-trip to picnic beside a river. In these essays Goytisolo shows he is well-informed and versed in several theories of the novel. In later years he has rejected these essays as immature and unworthy of being republished under his signature. This is unfortunate, because for their time and place they were lucid, courageous, and vibrantly written.[3]

The voluminous production of novels committed to social realism has been ably documented and studied by Pablo Gil Casado, who convincingly defends the importance of this kind of literature, years after the writers themselves came to consider it discardable. While many of these works pandered to the lowest common denominator and established black-and-white oppositions between the wicked, decadent upper class and the exploited, noble proletarians—producing pamphlets more than works of art—it is easy to name many novels of the period well worth reading today. To mention only two, Jesús Fernández Santos's *Los bravos,* published in 1954, is a kaleidoscopic reconstruction of life in a small village, where the aging chieftain and a young doctor lock horns for the meager spoils of an impoverished economy and a suffocating web of human relations. Rafael Sánchez Ferlosio's 1956 *El Jarama* re-creates a day in the lives of the locals and vacationers on the banks of the Jarama River, a location well known as the scene of a protracted and bloody battle during the civil war. It weaves the many threads of its story, mostly voices seemingly caught in trivial chatter, to reveal, beneath a surface of boredom and aimlessness, the possible interdependence and solidarity of the many characters of the novel, including the river itself and Death.

It is in this context, at a time when writing could constitute a form of political action and personal commitment, that Goytisolo wrote and published his first novels. To understand them we must remember that they were meant to be read as critical mirrors of society and expected a reading where each word would resonate with allusions to contemporary situations. One of the most debated and influential books of literary criticism of this period was José María Castellet's 1957 *La hora del lector* (The Hour of the Reader), which liberally quotes Sartre and Camus, and provides examples from Dashiell Hammett and Ernest Hemingway. Castellet's main claim is that in truly contemporary literature the omniscient narrator, who expresses for Castellet the certain and monolithic values of bourgeois society, has faded away, replaced by an objective narration based on existential philosophy and behaviorist psychology. Characters cannot be defined, only observed in action; people should not be analyzed, but their choices should be presented to readers who can then reach their own conclusions. The narrative voices of these novels tell only what a camera would show in a film. Writers who have grown sophisticated about their craft can offer readers more freedom, presenting them with a challenge, a world to re-create and decipher. But since ideal readers do not abound, and the writer should above all be socially responsible and talk about everyday life, obscurity and complexity should be tempered by prudence. It was a generous program, but it made compulsory and exclusive techniques which had worked well in the past and were already part of that past. Nothing contributed more to deflate Castellet's arguments than the meteoric appearance in 1962 of *Tiempo de silencio* (*Time of Silence*), a novel by a psychiatrist, Luis Martín Santos. Here the narrator colored every sentence with his immense wit and irony, impressive learning and demanding syntax. It was immediately recognized as one of the best Spanish novels of the century. The hour of the reader was over, and then came the age of language.

Writing from France: Structuralism and the Focus on Language

In 1953, the year in which Goytisolo traveled for the first time to Paris, Roland Barthes (1915–1980) published the seminal *Writing Degree Zero*. This book was at the forefront of a new wave of structuralism, a method that concentrates on systems and codes and is more interested in how meaning is produced than in meaning itself. Reaching back to the work of Russian formalist critics in the early decades of this century, it developed and applied ideas first expressed with authority by the Swiss linguist Ferdinand de Saussure (1857–1913). He introduced sharp and useful distinctions between the evolution of language through time and the way it works at any given moment, as a self-contained system that provides meaning to human utterances. Thus, when we talk, each of our words is recognized by our interlocutor as distinct from many others with similar sounds, not confusing, for example, *novel* with *navel*. Also, the interlocutor can understand the subtler difference in the meaning of the word *novel* when used to mean "a novel writer," that is, a new or original author, and in "the writer of a novel." Language, then, exists as a shared set of rules, a system of oppositions, and a network of codes speakers have internalized. Words are nothing more than arbitrary sounds—different from one language to another or in the same language from century to century—that point to a place in a system, as masculine, for instance, or singular, or a verb. The acoustic image or signifier, for example the word *horse* or *tree*, has as its referent not a real horse in a pasture or a tree in the woods but the image of a horse or a tree, also part of a system of images that differentiates, for example, a horse from a mule, and a tree from a shrub. Literary critics applied these observations to uncover in different texts the expression of the same structure, most effectively in the minute analysis of folktales by Vladimir Propp (1895–1970) and of myths by the French anthropologist Claude Lévi-Strauss (b. 1908).

For writers such as Goytisolo who had been following Sartre's call to a committed literature, in which the ills of society and the evils of human condition could be held up to scrutiny, structuralism offered a sobering look at the unexamined instrument of their task, language. Significantly, sections of Barthes's *Writing Degree Zero* appeared in 1947 in the newspaper *Combat*, the same year in which Sartre published *What is Literature?* Both books begin by examining the question "What Is Writing?" While for Sartre the ideal writer decided to stand apart from the routine of unexamined life and demand justice, truth, and freedom, Barthes pointed out that writers were forced to immerse themselves in the social aspects of life because they use language. "It is impossible to write without labeling oneself" (1), he asserts, because literature is an institution and language a horizon, each setting limits to choice. Every choice a writer makes—to write a novel or a sonnet, to be realist or surrealist, to focalize the action through a man or a woman, a peasant or a university professor—is significant. To write is to use a system set up by others, a system that reflects values and preferences of the past. Barthes's main argument against Sartre's is that supposedly revolutionary authors, because they depict society's ills, nevertheless use traditional resources of the nineteenth-century novel, created mostly by and for the bourgeoisie. A fresh new style, an author's signature, is not enough because for Barthes this style is mostly a closed personal process, with biological and biographical origins. The author, then, does not choose language or style; he only makes choices within the frontiers imposed by them. The materials writers use come heavily loaded: "Language is never innocent: words have a second-order memory which mysteriously persists in the midst of new meanings" (16). Marxist writers especially, Barthes continues, have developed a language of knowledge and value judgments that ignores the quagmire on which it is based and reduces the writers' choices to joining or not joining an institution. But any writer who uses "good French" is already caught up in a tradition that continues talking through her or him. If one is not to fall into silence, yet wishes a truly new form of literature, a solution may be to question what is expected of "literature" and to denude the text as much as possible of the rhetoric that is only there to guarantee a place within the literary realm. The new ideal in writing is to keep the imposition of the past reduced to a minimum.

Goytisolo in the late 1950s and early 1960s immersed himself in the study of linguistics and structuralism. Barthes's ideas had by then prevailed over Sartre's in many French intellectual circles. A vigorous and remarkably intelligent scholarly journal applying structuralism, *Tel Quel*, was founded in 1960, and Lévi-Strauss published two masterpieces, *Tristes tropiques* in 1955, and *La Pensée sauvage* in 1962. Goytisolo realized he was not only trapped by Spanish history but also by the history of Western literature and the limitations of language. His novel of 1966, *Marks of Identity*, begins a process of willful manhandling of the novelistic genre, in which ultimately characters, story line, correct syntax, and readers' expectations are ignored and frustrated. In the process, he discovered kindred spirits in the Spanish tradition, among them the author of *La Celestina*, Fernando de Rojas (1475 or 1476–1541). Goytisolo reviewed for the weekly *Triunfo* in August of 1975 a book that Stephen Gilman had published three years earlier on *The Spain of Fernando de Rojas*. Goytisolo's essay ends with an important idea, expressed as an afterthought and separated from the rest of the essay by three stars. He approvingly quotes Gilman's insight that Rojas had to express his rebellion against the world and Spanish society in a language that included a celebration of what he repudiated, making it difficult if not impossible for him to separate what belonged to "us," marginalized by race and religion, from what belonged to "them," secure in the centers of power of the nation and the church. Goytisolo goes on to affirm that this difficulty is not experienced exclusively by the Jews converted to Christianity in Spain, but of all those who conceive of their own language as a foreign territory. This crucial passage should be quoted in full.

This is a dilemma, I would say, that is not exclusive to *conversos*, but instead it concerns all non-conformists and rebels who conceive of the language in which they write as an alien territory—occupied by the defenders of the omnipresent official ideology: a territory plagued by webs, tethers, and traps through which one must advance taking infinite precautions and exploring it with great care, before placing there in turn numerous contact mines and time bombs destined to explode later in the hands of unwary readers. When I say this, I would like it to be perfectly clear that I am not just presenting a theory. My personal experience in fact coincides, centuries later, with the author of *La Celestina*. Forced to distrust one's own language, or better still, to think against it, the rebel, today as in the past, struggles to instill into his territory an atmosphere of subversion — ideological, narrative, semantic — that erodes and depletes it. (*Disidencias* 33–34, my translation)

We will see later how this desired triple subversion—ideological, narrative, and semantic—resulted in two of the most inventive and intelligent novels in contemporary Spanish literature: *Count Julian* and *Juan the Landless*.

Writing in a Democracy: The Marketplace, the Collapse of Ideologies, Postmodern Society, and Mysticism

In 1975, after thirty-six years at the helm of Spain and a dramatic, prolonged agony, Generalísimo Franco died in the belief that his legacy was a centralized, subdued, and conservative country. Yet the forces for regionalism, innovation, and reform surged immediately after his death and led an admirably smooth transition into democracy. The national fervor of Catalonia, Galicia, and Andalusia flourished, and capitalism boomed under the encouraging eyes of the moderately socialist government, while a new sexual freedom uncovered with a vengeance what only a decade before was unthinkable and forbidden. Once Franco's government was gone, Goytisolo needed to look for other targets, since he could not conceive of a literature of complacency and celebration. As he wrote in an essay entitled "De la literatura considerada como una delincuencia" ("Of Literature Considered as a Form of Delinquency," included in *Contracorrientes*, 1985), during Franco's dictatorship he was a delinquent in the eyes of Spanish authorities—an immoral and unpatriotic agitator—and some of his books were banned. This meant that his work was an effective irritant and touched a nerve. With the advent of an open and democratic society, explains Goytisolo in this essay, the heterodox becomes comfortable, literature circulates freely, and the writer is no longer considered a criminal. Perversely, writers holding unusual positions are searched for as marketable commodities, as "amables portavoces de una oposición domesticada y rentable" (*Contracorrientes* 183, "lovable speakers for a domesticated and cash-producing opposition"). Goytisolo has lined up in this sentence words he despises: to be lovable is also to be ineffective, for to him artistic truth must have a revulsive element and the messenger cannot escape its effect; to be a speaker for a cause is to annul the self and curb the independence of the questioning mind; to be domesticated, integrated into a house and family, saps the energy of spontaneity and deflects the wisdom of instinct; and to sell oneself on the lecture circuit or late-night talk shows is to become an accomplice of an industry that dilutes serious issues into frivolous entertainment. While society has become permissive, it has not eradicated injustice, racism, sexism, and xenophobia. Goytisolo calls for writers to continue their dissidence by speaking as Gypsies, blacks, workers, women, adolescents, homosexuals, and transgressors of the literary canon—"as one of them" and not "for them," that is, not just assuming their defense while remaining in a situation of safety, as a white male intellectual, but sharing their inferior standing. Goytisolo has been consistent with his ideas, firing his salvos in Madrid's daily *El País* and publishing uncompromising novels, but avoiding in his home base of Marrakesh the limelight and glamour of intellectual circles in Paris, Madrid, or New York. His collaboration with Spanish television has been a series of sympathetic and perceptive reports on the Arab world. His disdain of the marketplace is widespread in his novels but prominent in *Makbara*, a novel of 1980, where the traditional Arab market and oral tradition are favorably contrasted with the impersonal and exploitative mechanisms of modern commerce.

Around the time that the Spanish dictatorship ended—for once the peninsular clock synchronized with the rest of Europe—modernism expired. The grand and universal language of progress, technology, and certainty was replaced by the multiple chatter of postmodernism, where playfulness, skepticism, indeterminacy, and weak truths—truths that do not wish to expand to the whole universe—prevail. The anxiety modernist authors such as James Joyce (1882–1941) or Franz Kafka (1883–1924) felt at the fragmentation of the world, and their positing of a behind, beneath, or beyond where Truth resided, only glimpsed briefly in an epiphany, receded, replaced by a celebration of this fragmentation as a possibility for the existence of diversity within society and even in the individual self. Anxiety of influence, the call to displace the past, and the need to be in the avant-garde gave way to an embracing and recycling of any useful material from the past, most often wrenched out of context without regard to its historicity, the rigid order of the museum displaced by the simultaneous availability of the supermarket. The mechanical reproduction of works of art has become familiar in a world in which film and television provide some of the most intense aesthetic experiences for millions of people.

Goytisolo moved into this new perception of the world with characteristic creativity and depth in his novel *Paisajes después de la batalla* (*Landscapes After the Battle*), published in 1982. Here the narrative advances by the accumulation of small and loosely interconnected texts that present with obvious joy the breakdown of traditional order, as we will study in detail in chapter six. At this point, though, we must consider two terms brought into vogue by the philosopher Gilles Deleuze and the analyst Félix Guattari in their co-authored books *Anti-Oedipus: Capitalism and Schizophrenia* (1972) and *A Thousand Plateaus* (1980). These two terms explain much in Goytisolo's work: deterritorialization and nomadism. For Deleuze and Guattari, desire is the most radical impulse, flowing in constant transformation and behaving like a machine, indifferently transforming one form of energy into a variety of results. All sorts of power, among them capitalism and psychoanalysis, attempt to control, subdue, and reduce desire, creating legitimate territories set off from excluded zones, establishing prices and rewards, labeling the mind as sane or insane, defending the limits of private property and social propriety, and causing the individual to occupy a restricted and rigorous niche. Some writers, nevertheless—Deleuze and Guattari name Thomas Hardy, D. H. Lawrence, Malcolm Lowry, Henry Miller, Allen Ginsberg, and Jack Kerouac—"know how to leave, to scramble the codes, to cause flows to circulate. . . . They overcome a limit, they shatter a wall. . . . [They show] a violence against syntax, a concerted destruction of the signifier, non-sense erected as a flow, polyvocity that returns to haunt all relations" (*Anti-Oedipus* 132–33). Goytisolo highlights this urge to rescue his own desires from external shackles. His violence against syntax, concerted destruction of the signifier, and polyphony of haunting voices are related to a repeated need—because the process of liberation from all territories repeatedly fails—for overcoming limits and listening attentively to the flow of his emotions and desires. Because this need is deep, he still had a topic or a cause when Spain became democratic and encouraged diversity. He had become free to pursue a deeper and more radical search.

In *A Thousand Plateaus*, Deleuze and Guattari propose the nomad as a figure that represents a possible liberation from the restrictions of contemporary life. Situated in an interstice between established civilizations, nomads roam without roots, complex hierarchies, or accumulated history. Adapting to changing conditions, they constantly search for a better place and on their way plunder from others what they need but do not produce themselves. While nomads appear insignificant when seen from large cities, China and Rome were humbled and reinvigorated by them. They do not respect frontiers or conventional authority. Goytisolo identifies this nomadic spirit with the Arabs and calls at the end of *Count Julian* for a renewed invasion of Spain from Africa.

The desire to fell the tree of authority, ideology, and genealogy works its way out from these territories with irony, play, and idleness. It turns from an external and massive revolution to an examination of the mind. In the same way in which Barthes called for revolution in writing, and not only in the fictive world represented by a traditional form of the novel, Deleuze and Guattari point to the necessity of a transformation of the individual who does the writing and plans the revolution. Without this previous or simultaneous personal change, all other changes become frozen again into restrictive institutions and unexamined categories. Goytisolo recognized this danger early in his career and made of this insight a challenge to his readers not to fall into a complacent aesthetic enjoyment of his work, but to examine instead their own stages of sedentary rot or nomadic freedom. Many of his startling departures from traditional novelistic form are distancing and awakening techniques, in the tradition of German dramatist Bertold Brecht's (1898–1956) "alienation effect."

In a consistent and logical path, Goytisolo has continued his quest by exploring the language of mysticism. Mystics recognize no higher authority than their own hard-won experience, lament the insufficiency of language, and disdain the usual signs of prosperity and success. Because of this contempt for authority and status, they often run into trouble with authorities. In two of his latest novels, *The Virtues of the Solitary Bird* (1991) and *Quarantine* (1994), which will be discussed in detail in chapter six, the great poets of the Sufi tradition, the representatives of Islamic mysticism and of Spain, especially Saint John of the Cross, lend Goytisolo the ability to speak of the unspeakable, to look death in the eye, and to proclaim his insight into a form of truth that at last makes him free from the original sin of his signs of identity.

The Transcultural Hero:
The Search for Models of Unruly Behavior

Although Goytisolo's path has been a search of transformation and growth, some characters reappear in his writing. Later in this book we will analyze them in their specific contexts, yet it is essential to have a general sense of their importance first.

As mentioned in the introduction, for Goytisolo the thrill of attending university came from discovering other students and a few professors who agreed with the criticism he had generated from his own experience. From a social class—the upper middle class—he glided into a group that is frequently called "the intelligentsia." Belonging to this group does not depend on income or blood, but on education. Broad information, a critical stance, an active imagination, the practice of polemical thought, and a keen desire to understand the world in all its complexity lead intellectuals to question the univocal assumptions of their own social classes and to understand opposing viewpoints. In *The Young Assassins* and *Marks of Identity,* Goytisolo's characters receive from their reading and conversation snippets of information that confirm to them the existence of a possible better world. Goytisolo's experience conforms with what the German sociologist Karl Mannheim describes in *Ideology and Utopia*:

One of the most impressive facts about modern life is that in it, unlike preceding cultures, intellectual activity is not carried on exclusively by a socially rigidly defined class, such as priesthood, but rather by a social stratum which is to a large degree unattached to any social class and which is recruited from an increasingly inclusive area of social life. This sociological fact determines essentially the uniqueness of the modern mind, which is characteristically not based upon the authority of a priesthood, which is not closed and finished, but which is rather dynamic, elastic, in a constant state of flux, and perpetually confronted by new problems. (156)

One could add that the intellectual world is also an international social stratum, which would explain why Goytisolo's arrival in Paris so invigorated him. He attended dinner parties with writers and philosophers who shared his concern for freedom in Spain. His critical reporting found its way into *L'Express, France Observateur, Les Temps Modernes, Le Nouvel Observateur*, and *Le Monde Diplomatique*. Still, the positive portrayal of the intellectual will not survive *Marks of Identity*. His intellectuals in later novels are either isolated, working in small libraries, cut off from meaningful dialogue with the present and the past, or ridiculous, vain, and superficial. This does not mean that he does not continue to incorporate into his work the research of scholars he admires, such as Américo Castro or Luce López Baralt, both distinguished critics who have demonstrated the fundamental importance of the Muslim world to Spain. Nor does it mean that he does not speak with other intellectuals who have long been his friends, such as the Mexican novelist Carlos Fuentes, or with literary critics. As many other students of his work and I can testify, Goytisolo is generous, cordial, and supportive, an author who understands from the inside the intricacies of criticism and its difficulties. Yet, his later novels do not portray situations in which a group of intellectuals accomplish anything useful, as one could find in novels by José Lezama Lima or Julio Cortázar in Latin America or Luis Goytisolo and Carmen Martín Gaite in Spain. This may well reflect simply that the modernist highbrow has become tiring, as an emblem of how culture lost its common touch by insisting on a great divide between an elitist "high" art and art's degraded popular and commercial manifestations. But there may be a further significance to this shift: a wish to leave behind completely any sort of exclusive posturing. Karl Mannheim diagnosed this problem lucidly early in this century, proving that Goytisolo is far from an isolated case in space or time:

> This ability to attach themselves to classes to which they originally did not belong, was possible for intellectuals because they could adapt themselves to any viewpoint and because they and they alone were in a position to choose their affiliation. . . . This voluntary decision to join in the political struggles of a certain class did indeed unite them with the particular class during the struggle, but it did not free them from the distrust of the original members of that class. This distrust is only a symptom of the sociological fact that the assimilability of intellectuals into an outside class is limited by the psychic and social characteristics of their own . . . the fanaticism of radicalized intellectuals should be understood in this light. It bespeaks a psychic compensation for the lack of a more fundamental integration into a class and the necessity of overcoming their own distrust as well as that of others. (*Ideology and Utopia* 158–59)

This impossibility of completely assimilating oneself into another class is manifested throughout Goytisolo's writing. In spite of the wishful thinking implied in the title *Juan the Landless*, and the author's displacements to France and northern Africa, as long as he wishes to exist as Juan Goytisolo, he is in part determined by circumstances that connect him to Spain and a privileged education. Even his oppositional stance does not free him from being a Spanish intellectual; rather it brings him closer to what he rejects than if he just walked away into a horizon of silence and oblivion. By becoming a much-too-visible text, the context engulfs him with renewed strength. This is probably the reason why intellectuals such as Professor Ayuso of *Marks of Identity*, who are incarnations of the decanted best of his own culture, are replaced in later novels by a new sort of intellectual hero who rejects fundamental tenets of his own culture, is fascinated by another culture, and seeks to immerse himself in that other culture. Three examples can give us here the mettle of these new figures, two of whom appear in *Juan the Landless*: T. E. Lawrence (1888–1935) and Charles de Foucauld (1858–1916). The third is José María Blanco White (1775–1841).

It is easy to see why Thomas Edward Lawrence's complex life would fascinate Goytisolo. From its very start, it was marked by rupture and pretense. His father, Sir Thomas Robert Chapman, left his wife for his family's governess, with whom he had five children—among them Thomas—and settled in Oxford under the assumed name of Lawrence. Thomas eventually became a student of archaeology, architecture, and history at Oxford and began his studies of Arabic while visiting Syria and Palestine. At the time, these activities had all the glamour created by the expansion and consolidation of the British Empire. He worked as an archaeologist in different parts of the Middle East from 1910 to 1914, when World War I launched the contemplative scholar and antiquarian into a position as an intelligence officer. Because Turkey was an ally of Germany, the British thought that a rebellion of the Arabs against the Turks would weaken Germany and the resulting Arab dominions would shift to Britain's column. Lawrence, therefore, participated actively in the Arab revolt against Ottoman Turkish rule, helping decisively in the campaign that led to the entrance of the Arab troops into Damascus in October 1918.

These events have been re-created in the film *Lawrence of Arabia* (1962), directed by Sir David Lean, and images of this filmic Lawrence reappear in the pages of Goytisolo's *Juan the Landless*. The film derived many aspects of its glorified and romantic hero from Lawrence's own account of his Arab expeditions in *The Seven Pillars of Wisdom* (1926, private edition; 1935, general edition), but it cannot convey the depth of anguish contained in the brief first pages of chapter one, where Lawrence speaks of his double life:

Pray God that men reading the story will not, for love of the glamour of strangeness, go out to prostitute themselves and their talents in serving another race.

A man who gives himself to be a possession of aliens leads a Yahoo life, having bartered his soul to a brute-master. He is not one of them. He may stand against them, persuade himself of a mission, batter and twist them into something they, of their own accord, would not have been. Then he is exploiting his old environment to press them out of theirs. Or, after my model, he may imitate them so well that they

41

spuriously imitate him back again. Then he is giving away his own environment: pretending to theirs; and pretenses are hollow, worthless things. In neither case does he do a thing for himself, nor a thing so clean as to be his own (without thought of conversion), letting them take what action or reaction they please from the silent example.

In my case, the effort for these years to live in the dress of Arabs, and to imitate their mental foundation, quitted me of my English self, and let me look at the West and its conventions with new eyes: they destroyed it all for me. At the same time I could not sincerely take on the Arab skin: it was an affectation only. (31–32)

These chilling lines may explain Lawrence's subsequent abandonment in 1922 of his position as an adviser at the Colonial Office and his search for a life of his own, living most of the rest of his lifetime under assumed names, first Ross and later Shaw, as an enlisted man in the Royal Air Force and the Tank Corps. Of course, his pseudonyms were well known, and he kept up with his literary friends. He did not neglect literature, receiving special satisfaction from the success in America of his 1932 translation of Homer's *Odyssey*. He remained, nevertheless, a strangely marginal person, overshadowed by his legend and perceived as a misfit both by his friends in high society and those in the barracks. He was fascinated by mechanics and speed, participating in the development of high-speed boats and driving his motorcycle, on which he met his death when it went off a road.

Jeremy Wilson, in his long and detailed authorized biography, *Lawrence of Arabia*, speaks only briefly of Lawrence's unusual practice in his later years, revealed by the *Sunday Times* in 1968, of having himself flogged, observed, and otherwise disciplined. Lawrence probably wished to expiate, and at the same time re-create, a homosexual rape he suffered while briefly imprisoned at Deraa in 1917. In a letter of 26 March 1924, he writes:

I'm always afraid of being hurt: and to me, while I live, the force of that night will lie in the agony which broke me, and made me surrender. . . . I gave away the only possession we are born into the world with—our bodily integrity. It's an unforgivable matter, an irrecoverable position: and it's that which has made me forswear decent living, and the exercise of my not-contemptible wits and talents.

You may call this morbid: but think of the offense, and the intensity of my brooding over it for these years. It will hang about me while I live, and afterwards if our personality survives. Consider wandering among the decent ghosts hereafter, crying "Unclean, Unclean!" (Wilson 739)

Goytisolo appropriates the Lawrence myth and reinterprets him, choosing to stress the thrill of action, the power of assimilation, and the homosexual camaraderie present in his life, over the evident pain, distrust, and separation voiced by Lawrence himself. Yet I would not underestimate how this darker side may also have made Goytisolo's identification with Lawrence compelling. As we saw in chapter one, the episode when Goytisolo was sexually molested by his maternal grandfather at times may well have resonated in his memory with the cries of "Unclean, Unclean!" Also, both Lawrence's and Goytisolo's "passing" as Arabs is only an approximation. Here, as in the terrain of the in-between occupied by the transvestite and analyzed by Marjorie Garber in *Vested Interests*, it would be a misperception to assume that not completely transforming into the other—a woman, a man, an Arab—is a failure. This all-or-nothing demand corresponds precisely to the binary oppositions that the sexual or cultural transvestite questions. The words of Lawrence on this subject, already quoted a few pages before, are worth repeating: "the effort for these years to live in the dress of Arabs, and to imitate their mental foundation, quitted me of my English self, and let me look at the West and its conventions with new eyes: they destroyed it all for me" (Wilson 32). This is the corrosive and unsettling effect of these submersions into another culture or gender: the English self, the Spanish self, and the male self lose their moorings and appear as conventional, questionable, and replaceable. Montesquieu (1689–1755) in France with his *Persian Letters* (1721), and in Spain Cadalso (1741–1782) with his *Moroccan Letters* (1789) offer good examples of how powerful these interzones between cultures can become, and how they foster the critical thought associated with the enlightenment of the eighteenth century that founded the modern era. Lawrence and Goytisolo go a step further than Montesquieu or Cadalso, who only imagined seeing their own culture through foreign eyes. Lawrence in his white flowing gowns—both Arab and feminine—and Goytisolo in Marrakesh live out their writing in the space of history, inscribing their bodies, imperfectly and yet still powerfully, in foreign geography and culture.

A similarly complex evocation of a historical figure appears in *Juan the Landless* (124–29, 138–41), when the narrator visits the tomb in El Goléa (Algeria) of Charles Eugène Vicompte de Foucauld (1858–1916) and reads some of Foucauld's writings, reliving, as he puts it, "the fits of delirium and ecstasy of the Reverend Father Foucauld" (125). Foucauld's life is marked by an estrangement from France, a fascination with Africa, and a radical search for perfection. Briefly, these are some of the relevant facts: born to an affluent and aristocratic family in Strasbourg, Foucauld became an orphan at five and was raised by his grandfather, who provided affection and money but scarce discipline. He studied for almost two years in Paris with the Jesuits but loathed the stern and businesslike atmosphere of that school and was eventually asked to leave because of his lack of application. He then entered the army, studying to become an officer at Saint-Cyr and Saumur, managing through indolence and feasting to graduate eighty-seventh in a class of eighty-seven. In his bachelor's rooms in Paris and at his army post, he proceeded to squander much of a considerable fortune that his grandfather had willed to him when he was twenty. Sent to Algeria in 1880, he presented himself an introduced a lover as his wife, occasioning a scandal that brought about his dismissal from the army. Back in Europe with his lover, he read the news that his comrades in Algeria were involved in action and begged to be reinstated. Battle brought out unsuspected virtue, and he conducted himself with distinction during the campaign. Foucauld in turn was captivated by the beauty of the desert and the dignity of its inhabitants. He wrote later: "Islam has disturbed me deeply. The sight of this faith, of these souls living in the continuous presence of God, has made me aware of something greater and more true than worldly preoccupations" (Carrouges 21). He decided to explore the region—at that time mostly unknown to and off-limits for most Europeans—and made a perilous and unprecedented trip through Morocco, disguised as a Jew, calling himself Rabbi Youssef Aleman. Having to live in clothes different from his own, and experiencing, as an impostor, the kindness of both Jews and Muslims, his confidence in Christian European superiority was shaken.

On his return to France, where his accomplishments were amply recognized and where he published a book about his expedition, he experienced in 1886 a rebirth of his long-lost religious beliefs in Catholicism. Shortly thereafter he made a trip to Palestine, and on his return, in 1890, he became a Trappist monk, based first in France and then in Syria. But even the ascetic Trappist way of living seemed too lush for the life of self-effacement, contemplation, and penance he desired. The Trappists allowed butter with some meals! Luxury! They wanted him to become a theologian, even to make him an abbot! Worldly pride! He desired only to be the humblest of the humble. He left the Trappists in 1897 and went to Nazareth and Jerusalem, where he lived under an assumed identity as a servant in a convent. When he was recognized and his life again became pampered, he searched for a greater challenge. In Morocco he had admired the Moslem *zaouïa*, a place of prayer and hospitality for travelers and pilgrims and this became his model. After becoming a priest in France in 1901, he returned to Africa, this time to Beni Abbès in Algeria, where he led the life of a hermit, but in frequent and friendly contact with the French garrison and the native Moslem population. He soon came to be respected by both parties as a saintly and generous man. As Carrouges puts it, "Father de Foucauld was the man of frontiers. At Beni Abbès, he was on the edge of Algeria and Morocco. He was between the French and the Arabs, between the Christians and the Moslems" (161). Again, as in the case of Lawrence, what matters here is this precarious "in-betweenness" that becomes a scandal—the word *scandal* derives from a Latin word meaning *separation*—for groups whose claims to centrality and superiority are questioned. While the hermit had excellent relations with his former comrades in arms, even possibly helping them with intelligence reports, his disdain for possessions, his respect for the natives, and his calls for peace were an irritation. He wrote, for example, the following harsh words about the colonial enterprise:

What I see of these Sudan officers saddens me; they seem to be pillagers, bandits, free-booters. I fear this great colonial empire, conquered over a long period of time and capable of giving birth to so much good—moral good, genuine good—may soon become for us a source of danger that will make us blush even in front of the uncivilized; make the word French cursed and, unhappily, the word Christian, too; make people who were already in misery in greater misery still. (Hamilton 146–47)

Just as Goytisolo devoted himself to learning Arabic in order to share the life of the poor and uninstructed—an aspect of his life described by his wife Monique Lange in her autobiographical novel of 1982, *Les cabines de bain* (*The Bathing Huts*)—Foucauld spent the last years of his life living among the Tuaregs in a remote village, Tamanrasset, deep in southern Algeria and at the foot of the Hoggar Mountains. He produced a dictionary and a grammar of the Tuareg language, Tamashek, and became one of them: "He wanted *to think as a Tuareg*" (Carrouges 220, emphasis in the original). He was assassinated by a rival tribe, dying in a martyrdom he had courted for many years, a sacrificial victim in a story he had devised and in which he had come to belong. Goytisolo stresses Foucauld's self-abasement and quotes, among others, the following lines of the hermit's meditations:

one must pass by way of the desert, and tarry there in order to receive God's grace: it is there that one empties oneself, that one banishes everything that is not God . . . close every last book: never take up a pen: remain a servant . . . something tender, refreshing, consoling, gentle for all men: slaves, the poor, the sick, soldiers, wayfarers, the curious: not to fear contact with the natives or with their garments: to fear neither their filth nor their lice . . . the desire to experience love and the giving of oneself to the limit . . . I believe that is my vocation: to descend: poor, scorned, abject. (*Juan the Landless* 125–26)

Genet or Goytisolo could subscribe to such lines, which correspond to the "tender, refreshing, consoling, gentle" side of Goytisolo's work, but the Spanish author distrusts any appearance of conventional goodness. In fact, the narrator seems to side with the assassin, who is portrayed as strong and beautiful, and to scorn the hermit as deluded and masochistic. Yet the text as a whole is enormously complex: Foucauld is clearly seen as an alter ego who preceded Goytisolo to the desert, sharing many of his convictions and the same vocation to descend. Foucauld's search for abasement and his rejoicing in the face of suffering and expected martyrdom, his desire to expiate his sin and expunge his past, parallel Goytisolo's own quest to erase his signs of identity, explicitly shown in the rape and murder by an Arab of a child who represents Goytisolo in the closing pages of *Count Julian*. And, even if troubling and difficult, to be "tender, refreshing, consoling, gentle for all men" means also to be able to see the beauty and humanity of the assassin.

A third intellectual figure with which Goytisolo identifies is the Spanish priest José María Blanco White (1775–1841), some of whose works in English, written while in exile in England, were translated and published with an extensive prologue by Goytisolo in 1972. In these pages he describes how previous critics treated Blanco unfairly, denigrating his private life and ignoring the value of his writings. Blanco's sins include having a child while he was a priest (one child whom his critics multiplied into several), abandoning the Catholic church and joining first the Anglican and then the Unitarian church, writing against the Catholic church, being in favor of the independence of the American colonies, and freely questioning all kinds of assumptions. Born to a family of merchants in Cadiz, with Irish and Spanish ancestry, he perceived himself from the start as a misfit. He was educated at home and not allowed to mingle with other children. Destined to inherit his family's fortune and business, he hated commerce, played the violin, and loved the idle conversation of poets and scholars. The priesthood was a way out of his family's grip, but it also responded to his kindness, concern for others, and creative talent as a writer. During the wars that resulted from the invasion by the French in 1808, Blanco distinguished himself as the editor of an outspoken journal that ran afoul of official censorship. In 1819 he left for England, where he was well received, meeting many distinguished intellectuals in London and Oxford, where he lived for some time, and receiving official support for his publications about Spain and against Catholicism. Both in his beautifully written *Letters from Spain* (1822) and in his autobiography *The Life of the Rev. Joseph Blanco White, Written by Himself* (1845), he combined a highly critical mind with a courageous spirit, in writing also characterized by vivid and evocative descriptions. Some of the unforgettable events Blanco recalls include spiritual retreats, where drama and rhetoric obnubilated reason, and his adventures as a reader of forbidden books whose moment of glory is encountering several volumes of a French encyclopedia in the abandoned offices of the Inquisition. Blanco was also an accomplished poet, and one of his sonnets, "Mysterious Night," is frequently included in anthologies of English literature. Yet he was forgotten in his own country, until the recent rediscovery of his work in the last three decades.

Goytisolo writes at the end of his preface to Blanco's works: "Acabo ya y sólo ahora advierto que al hablar de Blanco White no he cesado de hablar de mí mismo" (98, "I end now, and only at this instant do I realize that while speaking about Blanco I have never stopped speaking about myself"). This strategy, to talk of the self through the interposition of a similar figure, speaks of the difficulty of directly confronting the writer's own truth, but also points out that however unusual Goytisolo may be, there are others who lived before him who shared his views and experiences.

Menéndez y Pelayo included Blanco White in his *Historia de los heterodoxos españoles* (History of Spanish Heterodoxes, 1911). A life defined as heterodoxy is defined from the outside, by a powerful institution that is strong enough to define orthodox thought, an institution from which the individual who falls from grace is punished with exclusion. The heterodox, in turn, do not simply walk away from the past, but become thorns in the institution's side. When in 1810 Blanco immigrated to England, he established there a newspaper called *El Español* (The Spaniard), revealing that in leaving his country he had become even more closely attached to it. His life is therefore one in which the struggle between the private and the social is won by the social because of the combined weight of family, education, profession, institutions, and memory. The major circumstance that defined him, as Blanco saw it, was to have been born in a country where Catholicism pervaded the life of the population, without any options, and based its power on the smothering of intellectual life, sexuality, and dissent. Blanco's denunciation of the refined manipulations of the mind by frenzied rhetoric and the gaze of a disperse authority—exemplified by spiritual retreats and confession—

finds an echo in Goytisolo's characters who are the victims of the assault of institutional strategies to keep them in a harmless niche.

Intertextuality, Montage, and Fragmentation

Goytisolo's novels place increasing demands on readers, who must be prepared to join in a creative experience. His novels up to *Marks of Identity* are traditional and require no more readerly input than a capacity to spot the occasional reference to highlights of Western culture, be they imbedded as a myth or sprinkled as names, quotations, and meaningful objects. From *Marks of Identity* on, the difficulties multiply and reading becomes a more challenging activity. References abound to less well known authors, interwoven in the text seamlessly, in a process of appropriation and recycling where footnotes or quotation marks would be an intrusion and an obstacle to the free flow of the text. Partly, this is because Goytisolo believes any text is mostly composed of quotations and references, and therefore isolating only a few voices obscures the presence of a thousand others in the lines claimed by the author as his own. The collective nature of language produces a text with many origins and intersecting cultures in an active dialogue—a polyvocal text—which Goytisolo makes central instead of glossing it over with the pretense of a single authorial voice. Partly, also, this meshing together creates a community where a medieval Spanish writer, a Sufi mystic, a seventeenth-century Spanish poet, a contemporary scholar, and Juan Goytisolo can confront their opponents with a composite voice, enjoying a degree of shared support that these heterodoxes, misfits, geniuses, or visionaries did not know in their own times. Intertextuality, then, becomes in Goytisolo's later novels more than simply the dialogue—willed or unwilled, explicit or implicit—among texts. The abundance of texts which, to an alert eye, seem to be flowing into Goytisolo's novels from somewhere else has a political purpose, the revelation of a tradition of resistance to the claims of an exclusive authority.

While some of the incorporated texts support the narrator's ostensible views, others are modified by their context into an ironic reading. One example that is characteristic of the procedure may suffice. In *Juan the Landless*, the narrator imagines a sugar plantation in Cuba, establish-

ing an opposition between the slaves—close to nature and sexually spon-
taneous, creative, and inexhaustible—and their masters, who have become sterile, artificial, and constrained. Hovering above reality, in a
heaven that evokes the Holy Family in the Greek Olympus, the owners
enjoy their family life. The father inquires about the slaves to his daughter Mary, who has been listening to the groans and pants emerging from
the slaves' quarters. She lies, reporting that she believes they are resting
after saying their prayers. The father, moved by this loyalty, decides to
go and bless them, but Mary, fearing what he would encounter, detains
him, as a modern Sheherezade, by reading a poem by the French romantic poet Alphonse de Lamartine (1790–1869). At first blush, this poem,
"Le Papillon" (The Butterfly), is frivolous fluff. All important to its reading is the good French accent and melodious declamation. The prestige
of France—the country where Latin American money, produced by exploiting the poor, was laundered by the glamour and veneer of high culture—lulls the father and distracts him from facing the truth of the
suffering and rebellious vigor of his slaves. To understand how Goytisolo
presses this poem into service, it is necessary to quote it in full:

LE PAPILLON

Naître avec le printemps, mourir avec les roses,
Sur l'aile du zéphir nager dans un ciel pur,
Balancé sur le sein des fleurs à peine écloses,
S'enivrer de parfums, de lumière et d'azur,
Secouant, jeune encore, la poudre de ses ailes,
S'envoler comme un souffle aux voûtes éternelles,
Voilà du papillon le destin enchanté!
Il ressemble au désir, qui jamais ne se pose,
Et sans se satisfaire, effleurant toute chose,
Retourne enfin au ciel chercher la volupté! (Lamartine 128)

(THE BUTTERFLY

Born with the Spring, dead with the roses,
On the wing of the breeze sailing a clear sky,
Hovering over the heart of budding flowers,
Dizzy with perfume, intense blue, and light,

50

To lose, still young, the color of the wings
And rise like a sigh to the eternal mansions,
This is the charmed destiny of the butterfly!
It is similar to desire, which never rests,
And never satisfied, touching lightly all,
Returns at last to find pleasure in heaven!)

My translation erases the difficulty the French text produces to the reader of *Juan the Landless*, in which foreign languages—English, French, Latin, Arabic—serve as obstacles to any threat of uniformity. The French here acts as a barrier that, in this case, separates the master, who understands the language and enjoys the poem, from the slave, who does not. But many more meanings arise from the placement of Lamartine's poem in the context of Goytisolo's novel. French is the language of culture as opposed to Spanish, which is used for the everyday in running the plantation. As such, French in Latin America becomes a language which distances and whisks away the sweat and toil of production. Fortunes are made in America and spent in Paris. The presence of these two languages used to separate two aspects of the plantation owner's life points to the problem of a culture not connected to its roots in daily experience, precisely the connection that Goytisolo labors to resurrect. Furthermore, the poem is truncated in *Juan the Landless*, in which only the first four lines appear. These verses describe the brief life of the butterfly and concentrate on its beauty, the brief mention of death couched in roses to soften its blow. The suppressed verses turn the poem into a meditation about the ephemeral nature of life and the persistent dissatisfaction of desire. That Mary reads to her father only the pleasant part of the poem does not surprise us and shows how literature can become an innocuous commodity when it is censored to make it enjoyable, a turn of events Goytisolo abhors. Many of the thorns, spikes, and other irritants found in his novels reflect his resistance to create what might be considered summer vacation reading or page turners.

The case of Lamartine's poem is especially ironic because this author has many qualities, aside from being a romantic poet, that could recommend him to Goytisolo. Lamartine belonged to an aristocratic and royalist family, grew up basking in privilege, studied with the Jesuits, started a promising career as a diplomat, and married a wealthy English-woman. Yet, he had loved a working-class woman in Naples, and after a trip to the countries of the eastern Mediterranean, when he visited Jerusalem, his outlook became radicalized. He participated actively in politics, abandoning poetry for the defense of republicanism and freedom, and distinguished himself during the Revolution of 1848. Much as other writers who Goytisolo brings into his pages and whom we have met before in this study, such as Lawrence and Foucauld, Lamartine turned against the comfort of his upbringing, preferring to see the truth rather than enjoy the myth.

Also, the indefatigable surge of desire described by Lamartine in his poem is a fitting description of Goytisolo's restless writing. At a later point in *Juan the Landless*, this butterfly shows up again, but this time it comes as a dark inhabitant of the night, still in search of total delight, circling around a light bulb, and is compared to the ideas that keep on returning and unsettling the mind of the writer. The ghost of those dismembered verses of Lamartine, therefore, is an important factor in the intertextual process, where the system of values that sustains the flight of the butterfly in a clear sky comes into conflict with the system of negations that gives rise to the nocturnal butterfly in the study-kitchen of the writer. This example offers a glimpse of the extraordinary density of Goytisolo's intertextual writing, its deep intelligence, and the demands of attention, knowledge, and insight he places on his ideal readers.

Most of the time, the texts brought together to form Goytisolo's novels are not allowed to retain even a semblance of independence. They are normally not neatly set apart, enclosed in quotation marks, or connected to footnotes, even if the author sometimes employs all these typographical techniques. Goytisolo prefers the montage, a procedure of superimposing images or contrasting them that has flourished this century in the collage and in film. The simultaneous presence or immediate succession of images or texts normally existing in separate realms forces the reader or spectator to ask why they have been brought together. Montage creates meaning indirectly and by stressing the importance of location. Police reports, newspaper clippings, letters, sections from other books, graffiti, advertisements, verses, descriptions of photographs, posters, and films appear looking slightly dislocated in their new context while acquiring the power of a museum object. In the same way in which a simple plate or knife, encased and labeled in an anthropological museum, speaks volumes about the civilization that created it, the texts Goytisolo finds and collects become representative and invite close scrutiny, sometimes revealing their depth, other times their inanity. The claims to power, wisdom, and privilege of empire, religion, and capitalism become suspect in Goytisolo's montage, just as a British judge in full court regalia would standing on a California beach. The effectiveness of this technique depends in many cases on the disruption of the original context. Reasoned arguments become absurd and unmotivated statements; complex images, snippets; persons, caricatures; and gray areas, sharp black and white. Goytisolo effectively borrows here from the tradition of the satire and the pamphlet, connecting with the great philosophes and writers of the eighteenth century, such as Voltaire and Swift. Their fight against absolutism, superstition, and dogmatism did seem to many at the time unreasonable—showing how completely reasonable ideas could be absurd, taking them to their logical extremes, focusing frequently on the negative implications of self-serving reasons—just as some readers today object to Goytisolo's strategies of fragmentation, ridicule, and exaggeration. We should not forget, therefore, that in this illustrious tradition of satire, which goes back at least to Greek comedy, behind the barb stand the ideals of freedom; that in a space where the powerful command dignity and define reason, the powerless often resort to the erosion produced by irony and wit to jolt readers into an alternate view of reality. In the next chapters, which describe in greater detail Goytisolo's novels and travel books, we will see how difficult it is to create this space of freedom, how long and arduous a struggle is involved, and how exceptionally rewarding are the results.

Notes

1. On the Falange, which still defined the Nationalist vocabulary in the fifties, see Stanley G. Payne's *Falange: A History of Spanish Fascism*. To understand how the Civil War continued to be remembered for many decades in vivid detail, see Ronald Fraser's excellent *Blood of Spain: An Oral History of the Spanish Civil War*.

2. See Oscar Barrero's book about the existentialist novel of the post-war era for a depressing sampling of the attacks against Sartre and the strong opposition against existentialism during this period.

3. Goytisolo's books of essays are admirable and merit more attention than I can give them in this book, especially for the insights they afford into his later Orientalism and his interest in mysticism. A detailed analysis of Goytisolo as essayist remains to be made and exceeds the boundaries of this study.

CHAPTER THREE

Portrait of a Degraded Society:
The Young Assassins and *Children of Chaos*

Children Alone and Rebels without a Cause

In 1953, when he was twenty-two-years old, Goytisolo wrote *Juegos de manos*, a novel full of rage, histrionics, and existential anguish. It achieved modest prominence when it was the finalist for the Nadal Prize of 1954, and it was translated into English as *The Young Assassins* in 1959. The main events in the novel are clear—a conspiracy to murder a prominent politician, the failure of the attempt, and the consequences of this failure—but the many characters and meandering dialogues provide the portrait of a segment of society more than sharply delineated psychological portraits of individuals. The story presents a group of university students and artists in Madrid who gather regularly to discuss the repression and injustice of Spanish society. They are painfully aware of their ineffectiveness, spending most of their time in activities that are only symbolically rebellious: they preach to the converted, get prodigiously drunk, lie to authorities, and enjoy the thrill of visiting the haunts of prostitutes and homosexuals. To their bourgeois parents, these incursions into the repressed side of politics, morality, and the self are upsetting, but no more than lapses in judgment and taste. To have an impact and consolidate the group, they decide to assassinate Guarner, a prominent figure of the establishment. One of the group, David, is selected to perform the deed, when he receives the lowest hand in a poker game. What he does not know is that, to test David's resolve, his cards were arranged by a sleight of hand (in Spanish, a *juego de manos*, the title of the novel). When David visits Guarner, posing as a journalist, the older man sees the gun but reacts only with dismay, calling David "My son." The young would-be assassin is unable to proceed with his plan and escapes. One of the leaders of the group, Agustín, decides to punish David's betrayal and murders him in his apartment. The landlady comes to bring David his dinner while Agustín is still there. Agustín, knowing

55

he will be recognized as the murderer, calmly eats David's dinner and then descends to a nearby bar to await the police.

The combination of a highly structured story and a proliferation of diversions that threaten to pull it apart remains a characteristic of Goytisolo's novels, as if he wants to contest authority at the same time he firmly controls his narrative. In the case of *The Young Assassins*, the plot incorporates ideas of Fyodor Dostoyevski's (1821–1881) *Crime and Punishment* (1866), Jean-Paul Sartre's drama *Dirty Hands* (1948), and Albert Camus's *Les Justes* (1949), while the punishment of the person who betrays the cause echoes John Ford's (1885–1973) masterful film *The Informer* (1935).

In Dostoyevski's novel the main character, Raskolnikov, sees the murder of a woman moneylender as a step toward obtaining the means which will allow him to help many, the benefits of his action outweighing, in his mind, his single act of violence. Surprised by the victim's sister, he kills her too, this second murder taking the life of a completely innocent woman. The suffering caused by his tormented conscience brings him to understand that evil is dangerous currency to pay for future good. Sartre, in *Dirty Hands*, explores the consequences of an act of violence committed for revolutionary reasons, and his main character commits suicide, much as Agustín in *The Young Assassins* gives himself up to the police, accepting his responsibility and conceding the futility of his act but also taking refuge in the greatness of his struggle.

Camus, in *Les Justes*, re-creates the discussions of the revolutionaries who killed the duke Serge Aleksandrovich, the czar's uncle and commander of the Moscow military district, by hurling a bomb into his carriage on 4 February 1905. The poet Kaliayev, who was in charge of throwing the bomb, did not go ahead in the first attempt because two children were riding the carriage with the targeted victim. Just as for David in *The Young Assassins*, the consideration of the humanity of their targets weakens the resolve of the conspirators. Much of the discussion in the play considers the difference between a gratuitous act of violence and a revolutionary act of the oppressed against the ruling class in an unjust society. From this point of view, the title of the English translation of Goytisolo's novel takes sides—making his characters assassins instead of revolutionaries—tipping a balance that is much more even in the original.

Ford's *The Informer* uses an event in the Irish resistance against British domination to show how an act of violence—the execution of an informer—can seem necessary if the collective safety is in danger, yet the camera follows with compassion the informer, making it impossible for viewers not to understand the tragedy of this situation. Thus, the plot of *The Young Assassins* is far from trivial or naïve and presents violence as a troubling alternative to the passivity of intellectuals. The sleight (or game) of hands of the Spanish title is also a reference, therefore, to the limited effect of writing in the broader social context, where the privileges of class, money, gender, and raw power are not undermined (they are at most annoyed), by a poem or a student newspaper.

To present his many characters in this novel, Goytisolo relies mostly on dialogue, but their voices are not distinct enough to become memorable. In a few cases, the narrator concentrates on one character, allowing a better view of him or her through direct reporting from the outside or moving closer into the flow of his or her consciousness. First, we encounter Luis, a rebellious son who despises his father, Don Sidonio, and mother, Doña Cecilia, even if he continues to live at home and to exploit his father's influence when necessary.[1] Luis's rudeness and sloppiness convey his defiance, a disoriented reaction to his parents' permissiveness and lack of greatness. His moment of glory comes when, during the family's Christmas party, his friend Uribe walks in drunk and drags him away to join the prostitutes who await them out in the street. The breakdown of communication between parents and children is repeated elsewhere in the novel, with the parents described as insignificant and smothering. This is especially the case with David, whose story in many details resembles what we know of Goytisolo's own life.

David lacks courage and conviction. He has grown up enjoying the care and affection of his mother, which he has tried to repay with good behavior and success in school. David considers himself unworthy of this privileged life and wishes to be punished and destroyed. As an adolescent, he had been attracted to Juana, a woman who did not like to be touched, a proper object of ever unsatisfied desire. When one day, sitting closely in a secluded garden, David dares to place his hand on Juana's knee, she burns his hand with her cigarette and he endures the pain without protest. Later he introduces Juana to his friend Agustín, who charms women and has become David's idol, and he even locks them into a room hoping they will make love. With these actions he experiences the exquisite suffering his masochism requires. Through the mediation of Juana, he offers himself to Agustín, who has awakened his homosexual longings. In David's diary, presented directly to the readers as part of the novel, he recalls that he is the descendant of an illustrious family in decadence after squandering the inheritance of his grandfather, who had grown rich in the Antilles. As a child, he had realized that the children employed in his family's business went hungry while he had to be forced to eat at home. He considers himself unfairly singled out for a life of plenty and feels guilty. His success in school is a sham that hides and increases his insecurity. His desire to forgo his privilege and redeem himself by becoming a victim grows. After rereading his diary, which describes a self he has come to despise, David has a thought that well describes Goytisolo's lifelong search: "He . . . felt the need to go down in the street to mix with people, to forget the class to which he belonged" (183). His apparent failure to murder the father figure, when he cannot pull the trigger and kill Guarner, involves a much deeper triumph, because this nonaction brings about his own desired destruction. He will finally be free of his spurious privileges, and his parents will be punished with greater pain, since the death of a son or daughter is in most cases the worst thing that could happen to a parent. Also, to die at the hands of Agustín is a culmination of David's masochistic and homosexual desire, as underscored when the sound of the bullet is compared to the crack of a whip.

In addition to the previously mentioned need for action, the guilt of the privileged, the desire to be punished, and homosexual desire, *The Young Assassins* introduces another important and recurrent topic in Goytisolo's work: role-playing as a way to uncover the deeper self. Readers should take care, therefore, not to confuse in Goytisolo the frequent role-playing of his characters with either hypocrisy or simple playfulness. In *The Young Assassins*, for example, one of the characters, Uribe, loves masks, mirrors, and cosmetics. As a homosexual living in a fragile closet, he is aware that his life is defined by hiding his true face, yet this constant pretense has made of him a consummate performer who enjoys his presentations and is able to see through his friends' rigid personalities. Idolized by his parents, who want him to become a painter or an actor, he turns against them when he sees them as suffocating and demanding. He develops a tortured relation with his mother and attempts in vain to estrange her from his father. After some years in Paris, he is back in Madrid, a failure in everything except his wild performances—becoming a scandal in a bar, dressing up in drag for a party—which make him a mystery and an entertainment for his friends. He is the one who performs the sleight of hand that assigns the losing cards to David, a childish trick with which he once entertained his parents suddenly transformed into an act of incalculable consequences. When he finds out that Agustín has decided to kill David, he runs to warn him. At that moment, when he is urging David to escape and begging to be forgiven, the thought runs through his mind—and he is awed by it—that this is his finest moment, the most dramatic, and his most memorable and effective performance. He feels himself a prisoner within his disguises, an actor on a set or a character in a book, but nevertheless it is while role-playing that he feels himself truly existing. Goytisolo here is expressing a disquiet that permeates his whole work, the bad conscience of the aesthete who, while doing a good action or defending the downtrodden, looks into the mirror and congratulates himself for his dramatic flair and sophistication, never knowing a true unself-conscious instant of solidarity.

Children of Chaos, written in 1954 and published the next year with cuts ordered by the censors—who did not appreciate profane language from the mouths of Nationalist soldiers—tells the story of one day in a region in transition. This region in the countryside is being evacuated by the Republican forces and occupied by the Nationalists toward the end of the Spanish civil war. In the vacuum of shifting power, the children in a camp kill the twelve-year-old Abel, a child who lives in a neighboring property called The Paradise. The children have become a wild gang, roaming the woods with their faces painted in colors encoding a hierarchy that reproduces the structure of the armies fighting around them. Here, as in *The Young Assassins*, role-playing becomes a performance with fatal consequences. The only voice of authority left is the radio, transmitting, from both sides, inflammatory messages that the children interpret as calls to action. They identify Abel as different and "execute" him.

The novel begins when a Republican soldier, Elósegui, who has decided to stay behind and join the Nationalists, finds the body of the murdered Abel and is himself attacked with a grenade by one of the children. From here the novel proceeds in several directions, its forward-facing narrative describing the arrival of the Nationalists, the gathering of the children, and their confession. Also, the novel uses a series of flashbacks to recall several stories: Elósegui's love for the schoolteacher, who dies during the bombing of a neighboring port by the Nationalist fleet, setting off the children's transgressions; and his previous love for another woman, with whom he is reunited at the end of the novel.

Abel's story is filled in as the novel progresses, from his being orphaned when his parents become casualties of the war, to his own death. Abel speaks and acts like a grownup, aged by events, becoming the confidant of older people and behaving with preternatural insight, even anticipating his own death. He lives with his great-aunt, Doña Estanislaa Lizarzaburu, in the manor known as The Paradise. She is a recluse who lives through recollecting moments of the past, much like a character in a Faulkner novel. She tells Abel the details about her unhappy marriage with an incompetent man who squandered their fortune, and about the death of her two boys. Another important character is a hobo, who curiously has invented a hair-styling gel made from cactus juice, an invention Goytisolo attributes to his father in his autobiography. Abel befriends him briefly, but then joins the boys from the camp, deserting the old man. Another strand of the story is Abel's friendship with one of the boys in the camp, Pablo, with whom he steals several objects, including two rifles, from two old ladies who invite them frequently to their house. They intend to sell the plunder and join the army, but Pablo takes off with the goods never to return. Abel, the victim, is marginalized in different ways— from his family, from the other children, and from his friends—singled out by circumstances to become the different Other that attracts the frenzied aggression of the homogeneous collectivity of children.

The comparison with *The Lord of the Flies* (1954) by William Golding (1911–1993), the English novelist and Nobel Prize winner for 1983, is compelling and instructive, because in both novels a temporary breakdown of authority challenges a group of children to imitate the structures of power with tragic consequences.[2] Golding's children are stranded on an island after the plane that carries them away from an atomic conflagration crashes, killing all the grownups on board. A twelve-year-old, Ralph, becomes the leader, proclaiming the importance of organized meetings, the building of shelters, and the maintenance of a fire which might produce enough smoke to attract a passing ship. He is aided by a fat and bespectacled boy nicknamed Piggy, who serves as the intellectual of the group. They are opposed by Jack, who leads the boys in hunting and grows increasingly fond of violence and power. One of the boys, Simon, is a Christlike figure who contemplates nature and is generous to all. The children, especially the younger ones, fear a beast they believe roams the forest, and they mistake the dead body of a pilot and his parachute, ruffled by the wind, for this creature. Simon, who discovers the truth about the pilot, is murdered by the children in a ritual frenzy, and Piggy is also killed in a turf dispute between Ralph and Jack. Ralph becomes the prey, and during the hunt for him they start a fire that attracts a passing warship that comes to the children's rescue.

Golding's novel concentrates more than Goytisolo's on the children and in the growth in them of the passions that lead to building a society and destroying it. The beast the little children dream of is their own id, the drive for survival that will stop at nothing and resorts to violence at the slightest provocation. All the children, with the exception of Simon, enjoy at some point or another the pleasure of destruction and the urge to kill. Golding clearly affirms that the evils of society stem from personal moral flaws that should be controlled by civilization. The trouble is that the grownups have not improved on the children and are themselves involved in a war with atomic weapons. In Goytisolo's novel, the same relation of old and young exists, because the rescuers of the children are in the final stages of a bloody civil war. The hobo tells stories of past wars, making the present only a continuation of a history of strife and violence. As in Golding's novel, in *Children of Chaos* the boys start a fire, establish a hierarchy, commit murder, and betray each other. The English translation of Goytisolo's title implies that the children act as they do *because* they are immersed in the turmoil of war, but the original Spanish title, which could be translated as "Shootout in Paradise" or "Mourning in Paradise," seems to indicate that even at the childhood level of human society and in the most idyllic of circumstances, violence and destruction will emerge and play an important role in history.

Evil, Memory, Self, and Other Obsessions

A closer look at these two early novels, *The Young Assassins* and *Children of Chaos*, proves rewarding in the context of Goytisolo's later work. One can find here the kernel of problems that the author will insistently examine during his career. In both novels a murder occupies the central point of the story line, and in both cases the victim is apparently innocent: David in *The Young Assassins* and Abel in *Children of Chaos*. They are expiatory victims, sacrificial lambs revealing the passions and smoothing the warps of human beings. Abel's name establishes a clear connection with the biblical Abel who is murdered by his brother Cain. Just as Cain is protected by God and has among his children the founder of towns, the assassins in Goytisolo's novels have justifications for their actions. Agustín kills David to uphold the value of commitment in the underground resistance, a violent movement that in his view is justified because it acts against a dictatorship that is, in turn, even more violently repressive. David's murder, then, is perceived by Agustín as an execution of a traitor, as a necessary punishment. David himself, resigned to his death, seems to believe in the importance of his death, as if the destruction of what he has come to represent—weakness, indecision, betrayal—were the only real contribution he could make. Similarly, Abel's death, again not resisted by the victim, unites the children against a person who represents for them a threatening otherness of higher culture, class, and economic standing. Both Abel and David make manifest in their deaths the network of power that is normally not easily perceived, veiled behind language, institutions, and ceremonies. For Goytisolo this established power is used for the benefit of a few undeserving people who give priority to the conservation and increase of their property and safety over the needs of a majority, a majority that has been fragmented into a profusion of minorities variously stigmatized to justify their lowly status. A reading of Freud's and René Girard's studies of the importance of sacrifice for the establishment of religion can be helpful in understanding the prevalence in Goytisolo's work of murder and destruction as rituals that illuminate the shortcomings of the world.

As mentioned before, both Golding and Goytisolo develop the concept that the faults of society can be found in the individual, but an important difference in the way in which they tell their story reveals a point of divergence. Golding only briefly touches on the background of his children, as if their minds were free to respond to the new environment of the island without the strong conditioning of family, country, and religion. Although there are some references to the comforts of the home, the discipline of the school, and the adventurous spirit of an imperial society, in general, the children appear to be discovering anew the same situations they left behind, not imitating but re-creating. In Goytisolo's novels many pages reconstruct the past of the characters, stressing the presence of history, that is, how in the present the mind sees, reacts, and interprets according to experiences, memories, and interpretations that each person carries into the present from the past. These reconstructions of the life history of each character are often clumsy and make of these novels a sprawling set of interruptions in which the main narrative frequently stops to allow a character to reminisce. Later, Goytisolo will find more original ways to make use of this idea, but the concept of any given instant as an unavoidable meshing of past and present will remain fundamental.

Finally, a question and a definition that will run through most of Goytisolo's writing are already present in these early novels: who am I? is a central concern for David and Abel, but they discover that they are defined from the outside, by others and by all they have inherited from their family, social class, and several types of conditions. Both David and Abel reject in part their given selves—David joins the resistance, Abel the roaming band of schoolboys—in an attempt to create a new and chosen self, but they encounter the resistance of memory, of the indelible traces that others still recognize and reject. David fails as a revolutionary; Abel cannot survive as a destitute child, and they are left dangling between home and goal, between being what they are and an ideal self, in a nomadic search that is punished by destruction and death.

Notes

1. The choice of name for this character—the same name as Juan Goytisolo's leftist brother Luis—can be seen as part of the often-conflictive dialogue the brothers have had through their novels and essays.

2. Goytisolo declares in an interview with Emir Rodríguez Monegal that he had not read Golding's novel when he wrote *Children of Chaos* ("Destrucción de la España sagrada" 46–47).

CHAPTER FOUR

A Documentary Obsession:
The Countryside of Níjar (1959) and *La Chanca* (1962)

Writing the Spanish Landscape: Other Contemporary Examples

When Goytisolo embarked on a three-day trek in the province of Almería, in the Andalusian region of southeastern Spain, he was retracing the literary steps of many travelers in the past who reported about landscapes, towns, and people that were unfamiliar to most of their readers. Some notable examples are José María Blanco White's letters about Andalusia, Richard Ford's (1796–1858) *A Hand-Book for Travellers in Spain and Readers at Home* (1845), and the many texts in which the authors of the turn of the century, such as Azorín, Baroja, and Unamuno describe their travels in Spain. Just before the civil war, in 1932, Luis Buñuel (1900–1983) filmed a documentary, *Las Hurdes, tierra sin pan* (*Land Without Bread*), which became a classic portrait of the pockets of primitivism and poverty found in the neglected rural regions of an industrial society. The two books most comparable to Buñuel's documentary are a narration by the 1989 Nobel Prize winner for literature, Camilo José Cela (b. 1916), *Viaje a la Alcarria* (1948, *Journey to the Alcarria*), and the collaborative *Caminando por Las Hurdes* (1960, Hiking in Las Hurdes), written by the novelists Antonio Ferres (b. 1924) and Armando López Salinas (b. 1925). It will be helpful to describe these last works before embarking on a study of Goytisolo's travel books, in order to understand better his unique contribution to this genre.

Cela was an avid traveler in his own land and wrote several books and many newspaper articles based on these local expeditions.[1] Three volumes of his *Obra completa* (Complete Works) contain accounts of some of his trips in Spain. *Journey to the Alcarria* is the first and the best of these, imitated later by other writers and by Cela himself, who never again attained such a concise, graphic description of an impoverished countryside as in this compact text, in which small towns and their inhabitants are portrayed with the irony of a city dweller but warmed by a charity similar to that of the Italian director Federico Fellini's (1920–1993) classic films and the best of Italian neorealism.

As an unnamed traveler leaves Madrid early one morning, he encounters a silent city, reeking of death, where "the mysterious black streetcars of the night carry in all directions their scaffolding on wheels; the conductors are men without uniform, men with a beret, silent as corpses, hiding their faces with scarves" (chap. two). The reference to the frequent disappearance of citizens at night during and after the civil war is clear, and is reiterated in other passages that only seem innocent and innocuous: "On their way to the slaughterhouse, sheep pass by, sheared, dirty, and with a red B painted on their backs" (chap. two). Spanish readers, who knew of the restraints censorship placed on authors, were experts at giving any text an ironic, metaphoric, or allegorical reading. Cela, as does Goytisolo later, knows how to play this game, less evident for a foreign reader who is not used to the rules of restricted expression and lacks the cultural context to unscramble the encoded passages. The red letter gives these sheep, destined for the slaughterhouse, away: they stand in place of the many Republicans, usually referred to as "reds," who were summarily executed during and after the civil war.

Leaving the city, Cela's traveler sets off on the road with no specific goal, getting a taste of freedom. In his walk of 6–15 June 1946, he rediscovers in the resilience and the grace of the country folk the complex fabric of Spanish history that persists untouched at a short distance from Madrid. On the other hand, the traveler observes that even though seven years have gone by since the civil war ended, the ruins remain and there are no signs of modernization in rural Spain. Remembrance of past greatness substitutes for the solutions of present problems.

The traveler meets a gallery of characters who with economy and grace come to life under his pen: a sad red-headed boy, a traveling salesman, a schoolteacher—all limited in their horizons but occupying with dignity their marginal spaces in life, much like the peasants Goya had painted over a century earlier. He also notices, without comment, the hardships of a primitive industrial production and scarce resources. But mostly the traveler enjoys his trip, even to the point of becoming worried by the pain this happiness will bring him later, when he has lost it, or by the restlessness this taste of freedom may bring to the routine of his daily life. The trip must end, and the traveler returns to the city on a bus, to reintegrate himself with his humdrum reality, in which most people are anonymous and lack the roots and tradition he has found in the country-side.

The writing of *Journey to the Alcarria* and its publication by the most prestigious intellectual journal, Madrid's *Revista de Occidente*, was an act of restoration of realistic vision, or at least a successful attempt to demonstrate that a gap existed between literature and the historical reality of Spain. Subsequently, many of the novels of the 1950s had a descriptive purpose, attempting to fill the void left by a bland, controlled, and willfully ignorant press. The map and photographs that accompany this book speak the authoritative language of geography and anthropology, heightening the narrative's illusion of reality.

Antonio Ferres and Armando López Salinas published novels that describe a landscape and the workers who live there. Ferres's *La piqueta* (1959, The Pickax; in this case, the workers live in shantytowns near Madrid) and López Salinas's *La mina* (1959, The Mine), unfortunately, are not able to substitute their good intentions for lack of character development and flat style. The travel book was more amenable to their talents, and with the example of Cela's *Journey to the Alcarria* and a few chapters they had read of Goytisolo's *The Countryside of Níjar*—both explicitly acknowledged in their introduction to their own book, *Caminando por Las Hurdes* (Hiking in Las Hurdes)—they set off to retrace Buñuel's expedition of the 1930s. The book's lack of novelty reveals there is nothing new to show after twenty years of Franco's government. When they set out, as they put it, to "contar España" (9, "tell about Spain," though the phrase may also mean "account for Spain"), the implicit claim is that things should be better, different, and less painful, but they are not. The few changes that do exist are not altogether improvements. They notice, for example, that tourists are starting to discover the more picturesque towns of the region, contributing to their economy. Yet one of the products the local merchants are selling is their ancestral jewelry, which is slowly disappearing into the hands of antiquarians and tourists. The travelers lack the easy irony of Cela and paint a heavy-handed portrait of squalor and misery. For them most conditions are awful, and life in poverty is degrading. Significantly, they often reiterate that children as well as dwellings all look alike, an observation that any local would reasonably assert could only be made by an outsider who does not know them well. The travelers are imbued with good intentions, explaining to the villagers that they are also poor and hard workers, because until peasants and factory workers learn to read, writers will be as poor as the villagers. The travelers chat, as they walk into a squalid town, about recent papal encyclicals. In spite of this partial blindness—or perhaps because of it—the region and the villagers come through with strong and moving personality, with deeper and more convincing life than any of the characters that Ferres and López Salinas created in their novels.

The Countryside of Níjar

Goytisolo's *The Countryside of Níjar* has many similarities with the two travel books just mentioned. *Countryside* opens, as they do, with a detailed map on which the wanderings of the writer are neatly indicated with a flow of arrows. Ten photographs accompany the eleven brief chapters, providing a visual confirmation of the truth of the narration. The narrator refers to himself most of the time in the third person, as "the traveler." He comes from the city for a brief three-day hike, a time frame with a long history in the esoteric tradition. In fact, like many initiates of the past, the traveler will experience a revelation and suffer a transformation. Contemplating the ragged, poor, and already more African than European landscape, talking with the people, reflecting on the history of the region, the traveler goes beyond mere tourism. More than an amused spectator, he is a moved advocate, a medium for an ignored netherworld. In a bar in Almería, at the start of his trip, he meets two men who, under the influence of wine and the beatific vision of a group of elegant women going by to a baptism, proclaim that Spain may not progress but is still the best country in the world to live in. The reader may suspect the coincidences here have the smoothness of invention, more than the ruggedness of reported experience. The baptism recalls the influence the Catholic church has had in Spain, extolling the spiritual benefits of poverty, obedience, and resignation. Yet at the same time the scene becomes a fitting symbol of the deep and indelible imprint this trip will leave on the writer. The women and their fancy attire display the marked differences of wealth, but a voice from the crowd, darkened by desire, shouts a lecherous comment, reintroducing the leveling force of sex.

The traveler sees some signs of progress, such as experimental farms, but mostly observes a depleted land where the people dream of Catalonia as paradise. The traveler becomes aware of his privileged condition—at least in the eyes of the people he meets—and observes the nobility and dignity of the workers he encounters, unshaven, raggedly dressed, yet with sharp minds and helping hands. In a happy coincidence, the brand of cigarettes the traveler shares often with the workers he meets is Ideales. Slowly, as the peasants, miners, potters, and other workers make their appearances, and the land itself displays its beauty, the traveler's ideals of justice for all and fair progress take root and demand that this region receive greater attention from the rest of Spain.

The narrative moves forward on the thread of the traveler's itinerary. On the way, brief encounters illuminate a whole life. An old man, vainly attempting to sell prickly pears in the market, reappears again later in the road, with his basket still full, and tells the traveler about the hard times he and his wife have experienced. There has been a drought for several years, the children have grown and left them, the best of the sons died, and his produce does not sell. Nevertheless, he does not allow the traveler to buy his prickly pears, knowing well he would feel degraded and demoted from merchant to beggar. After forcing the traveler to accept some of them as a present, reestablishing his dignity as a host, he nevertheless is forced by his poverty to accept the bill the traveler offers him. Yet he proudly refuses any pretense. Before snatching the money from the traveler's hand, he intones the psalmody of professional beggars, "Una caridad por amor de Dios" ("A charity, for the love of God"). Having performed his new job in good conscience, he walks away with his head upright and without looking back.

The traveler hitches a ride with Don Ambrosio, a man who is visiting his real estate properties. He takes the traveler to see the ruins of a mansion, abandoned by a family who left the region. Then they visit several of his tenants, who plead with Don Ambrosio their poverty, sickness, and needs. He moves around like a patriarchal figure, granting or withholding his mercy, familiar with all from the heights of his power. In a sense, Don Ambrosio is a hard worker, who has come here from Castile and is resolved to develop the seashore. He dreams of roads, tourism, progress. His main problem, as the traveler sees it, is that Don Ambrosio is an outsider and the people of the Almería province continue under him a destiny of subservience and dependency.

In chapter ten, the traveler takes a bus while a storm rages—useless water that only lifts clouds of humid dust—and returns to town, to meet again two men who celebrate the beauty of the country and the superiority of Spain over other nations. The traveler has seen enough to know that postcards and museums cannot solve poverty and lack of opportunity. While the two men ramble on about music and bullfights, sun and Gypsy girls, the traveler drinks wine and cries, prompting some children to assume that the traveler is in mourning for a death in his family. From baptism to funeral, from amused aestheticism to tears, the trip has gone far enough. In the eleventh and very brief chapter, the traveler leaves on a bus to Murcia and reads two Sunday newspapers that provide the usual mix of sports, regional news, and publicity. A person sitting next to him borrows one of the newspapers and points out that this year's production of olives will be higher than last year's. More than a closure to be interpreted—does it show some hope or is it an ironic reflection on the modest dreams of the peasants?—this final line is moving because the traveler has missed the news that most interested the local person, suggesting that the gap between the intellectuals of Barcelona and the inhabitants of the Níjar region cannot, after all, be closed with a three-day hike.

La Chanca

Three years later, in 1962, Goytisolo published, in Paris, *La Chanca* (translated into English with the same title, because it is the name of a neighborhood), in which he describes a visit to an impoverished suburb of Almería. There, on the craggy slopes of a hill overlooking the Mediterranean, about twenty thousand people survive in dreadful conditions. Most of them are unemployed and live in houses with no running water or electricity. There are no doctors available, and conditions are unsanitary. The resplendent whitewash on the walls of the dwellings, interspersed with splashes of intense blue or yellow, attracts the cameras of tourists and hides the poverty of its inhabitants. This travel diary, like *The Countryside of Níjar*, turns out to be a book of revelations.

La Chanca tells a compelling story. The narrator is in Paris and, to his surprise, misses the country he tried for so long to leave behind. He scans the newspapers for news from Spain and strikes ephemeral friendships with other immigrants with whom he shares nostalgic memories and revolutionary projects. One of these acquaintances, Vitorino Roa Cabrera, tells him about a younger cousin he has in La Chanca, Antonio Roa, and the narrator promises to visit him on his next trip to Almería. The narrator and Vitorino had been reminiscing about the beauty of Almería—the sun shining on the blossoming orange trees—and the variety of its geography. Vitorino fought in the Spanish civil war and is awaiting only the death of Franco to return home. The scribbling on a card of the name of his cousin for the narrator to visit could be simply a friendly gesture, but this action suggests that Vitorino is hoping to teach the nostalgic young intellectual a lesson, by forcing him to confront the harsh reality of La Chanca with his idealized picture of southern Spain. The name Vitorino, by the way, is unusual, since it sounds Italian and not Spanish, and it is clearly an allusion to Elio Vittorini, one of the most distinguished figures of Italian neorealism. Vittorini, as Vitorino may be doing here, recommended that young intellectuals mingle with workers and learn from them.[2]

A few months later, the narrator takes off for Almería in a despondent mood. On his arrival there, the bustle of the sun-drenched city, the spectacle of the street vendors and the sidewalk cafés have a balmy effect on his spirit, until he happens to sit next to three men who are boasting of their prowess with women, especially young prostitutes. The narrator feels sickened and recalls the reason he had to leave Spain, his rebellion against a pervasive baseness and corruption which he calls the Great Cancer of his country. It is appropriate to remember that 1962 also saw the publication of Luis Martín-Santos's (1924–1964) *Tiempo de silencio* (*A Time of Silence*), a corrosive and influential novel of the post-civil war period, in which the main character is a researcher investigating the proliferation of cancer. The comparison of the motherland with a body and of moral abasement with sickness is frequent in Goytisolo's work. In this case, the little-understood and often fatal progression of cancer serves to capture the traveler's dismay. As an exile and a writer he cannot do much more than report the evidence he finds when he tries to convey to Antonio Roa the greetings from his cousin in Paris.

Entering the neighborhood La Chanca, the narrator feels he has passed into a region where he is a foreigner. Sophisticated and affluent, well dressed and sporting sunglasses, he is out of place among the squalor of crowded houses, dirty and pestilent streets, and clothes mended so often they seem only a structure to hold together their patches. He encounters curiosity and distrust, but eventually finds Roa's house, only to discover that Antonio Roa had been taken away ten days earlier and has disappeared, probably into the hands of the police to punish him for his participation in labor unrest. Vitorino's card serves as a password, and the traveler is cordially received by Roa's wife, three children, and brother-in-law, Luiso, and his wife and mother-in-law.

Just as in *The Countryside of Níjar*, Goytisolo focuses with economy and great effectiveness on a few characters, giving us enough information to imagine their lives. The most important is Luiso's mother-in-law, who is delighted to meet someone who lives in France. She feels grateful that her son, Juan, found a job in that country. She has recently received a visit from French tourists who took photographs of her and her family. The visitor is shocked when he finds that Juan had died, shortly after his wedding, in an industrial accident in Grenoble, where he had been working close to a boiler in a job so dangerous no Frenchman would have accepted it. The woman has been mulling over this and other events for years, but only now has the chance to ask questions from an educated and well-traveled visitor. She tells the story of her husband, an exemplary worker who held to the belief that effort and honesty were essential virtues that would be rewarded. He stayed out of the conflicts and disorders of the civil war and therefore neither was punished nor reaped any reward. During the harsh 1940s, known as the years of hunger, he was forced to steal to provide food for his children. Repelled by a world where honest work is not enough, his spirit broken by his descent into criminality, he had taken to the bottle and drunk himself to death. The woman asks the visitor: To be good and honest, is that not enough? Admirably, there is no answer. The question is left to the reader to ponder.

Later in the day, the old woman experiences a revelation, and tears flow down her face. The visit of the narrator, who has joined the family in their meals, shared their stories, and treated them as equals, illuminates in retrospect the visit of the French tourists. She now sees that for them her poverty and sorrows were a picturesque occasion for a photograph and a reaffirmation of their own well-being. This explains why there are no photographs in Goytisolo's book, except for the one on the cover of the 1981 first edition in Spain, a stunningly beautiful view of La Chanca taken by Carlos Pérez Seiquer. There, a young woman in a light-green dress is hanging clothes to dry on a clothesline a few inches away from a luminously white wall. Rising above the flat roof of her house, other houses shine under the sun in a geometry of whites, blues, and yellows. An intensely red jacket hung to dry is echoed by two bright red doors and a red shutter. At the top, the houses blend into caves dug into the rugged brown rocks. It is all much too beautiful and can easily make us forget that in one of those small dwellings lives a crowded family in desperate conditions. Goytisolo has skirted the danger of aestheticism while at the same time avoiding making a pulpit of his book. The narrator is subdued, humbled by what he sees, and his only wish seems to be to share the thought-provoking experiences he had in La Chanca.

Luiso serves as his guide. He takes the traveler to visit an admired old timer, but they find him sick and despondent. Luiso offers a tour of the poorer parts of the district and afterward takes his new friend to a bar where they listen to the neighborhood gossip. They then return to Luiso's home, where they prepare a dinner with the many sausages the traveler bought. Later they go out again, this time to a bar where the whole family joins them and they all reflect on their problems. The traveler becomes melancholy and drunk, and believes he is back in Paris, reporting to Vitorino that Almería has lost its sun and fresh air. He is in fact in Luiso's bed, while his host sleeps on the ground.

If the narrator allows himself some strong opinions, they are in the matter of Almería's fate in Spanish history. From a period of splendor when it was Arab territory, it was stripped of its industry and natural resources, of its independence and self-determination under successive governments controlled by Madrid. Appendixes to *La Chanca*, a series of texts written by historians and other travelers, describe this path from splendor to misery, from exporter of cloth to exporter of cheap labor. Almería, affirms the narrator, is not a Spanish province, but a Spanish possession militarily occupied by the police (86). A postcolonial time, implies the narrator, can only begin when this internal colonialism is recognized and corrected. As an article in the Madrid newspaper *Pueblo* of 26 October 1961—included as another appendix to *La Chanca*— shows, there was not much hope at the time that his voice would be heard. The essay is subtitled "La Chanca. The most picturesque fishing village in the world" and proceeds to extol the beauty of the town, marred only by Gypsies and the rumors spread by bad literature. Postcolonialism exists when those colonized become aware of their situation and struggle to be free but the colonial center refuses to let go or recognize its nega-tive influence, and still exerts determinant power in the economy and culture of a region. Such was the case of La Chanca as Goytisolo saw it in the early 1960s in this slim book that can rightly claim the title of masterpiece.

Goytisolo's fascination with Almería, which he first visited in 1956, goes beyond the description of the postcolonial situation of a Spanish territory, as Fernando García Lara in 1987 rightly pointed out at a lecture given at a colloquium in Almería devoted to Goytisolo's work. He made of this depleted land, soon to be recolonized by real-estate developers and tourists, a symbol of his own self. It was not by becoming a French intellectual that he would find his authentic voice, but by adopting the Arab and African roots still present in Almería. In his later books, this stark geography will be transmuted into an alter ego, a double, a brother whose poverty, vitality, tradition, and beauty he will embrace without patronizing. There is much to be said in praise of these two travel books, in which the author takes second place to a region and a people hitherto forgotten. They are far from flat documentary efforts, being instead seamlessly constructed narratives, distinguished by their inventiveness, subtle use of symbolism, creative presentation of characters, and an en-lightened diagnosis of a historical moment.[3]

Notes

1. My description here of Cela's *Viaje a la Alcarria* is a modified version of what I wrote in pages 3112–13 of "Camilo José Cela," an article in volume thirteen of *European Writers: The Twentieth Century*, edited by George Stade.

2. In *Realms of Strife* Goytisolo gives a portrait of Vittorini (77–78) and adds: "Later his literary work would exercise a momentary influence on mine: when he read the Spanish text of *Campos de Níjar* he suggested the idea of extending it with a slight narrative plot and, in the light of his experiment in *Il Sempione strizza l'occhio al Frejus*, I wrote the fictional documentary *La Chanca*, the Spanish edition of which I dedicated posthumously to him" (78).

3. Similar virtues are only sporadic in *Pueblo en marcha. Tierras de Manzanillo. Instantáneas de un viaje a Cuba* (A People on the Move. The Lands of Manzanillo. Snapshots of a Trip to Cuba, 1962), where Goytisolo's enthusiasm for the Cuban revolution at that time produces an idealized and one-sided portrait of his visit to the Caribbean nation.

CHAPTER FIVE

La dolce vita: An Insular Society Parties on the Brink of Disaster

Disgruntled Intellectuals of the Late 1950s and Early 1960s

Among Spanish intellectuals, few films had the impact of Federico Fellini's (1920–1993) *La dolce vita* (1960). With an audacity censorship would not have allowed in Spain, the Italian film shows the despair some recognized on the faces of the oppressed poor and the indifference of the upper classes. The film presents an aimless society, in which a decadent upper class is oblivious to the problems of the growing urban poor that surround it. Marcello, the journalist who serves as the focus of the film, visits an urban development in Rome in a nightmarish descent into hell, but he and his rich companion use the experience as a mere opportunity to make love, borrowing a poor prostitute's bed. Marcello's idea of a revelation is a strip-tease, a skin-deep and public spectacle spurred on by a frenzy of individual and egotistical desires. The acerbic yet compassionate camera of Fellini pries behind the glamour of fast cars, parties, and fame. It finds violence, indifference, boredom, and suicide. Marcello's elegant nonchalance and jaded irony will be echoed by countless novels in Spain in which promiscuous heroes drink themselves into stupors, preferably in seedy locales and in the company of the lower classes, to protest quite ineffectively and try to forget the inanity and injustice of modern society.

The intentions were good and generous, a mea culpa that eventually led to an understanding of the need for more focused action, both in politics and in language, inasmuch as language helps to transmit and perpetuate stereotypes. At a time in which participating in oppositional politics was perilous in Spain and the examination of the individual psyche seemed a luxury, Goytisolo and others chose to describe a dysfunctional society, insular, unaware, and apathetic in the face of an approaching storm. Luis Martín Santos's *Time of Silence* (1962) is the most memorable of these novels, but there are other notable ones, such as Juan García

Hortelano's (b. 1928) *Las nuevas amistades* (1959, New Friends) and *Tormenta de verano* (1962, *Summer Storm*). In the first of García Hortelano's novels, an abortion serves as a pretext to bring together a group of young people who indulge in endless and pretentious conversation; in the second novel, the discovery of a woman's dead body on the beach of a summer resort triggers for some vacationers an existential crisis, but it is shallow and transient, no more than a summer storm.

To understand Goytisolo's novels of this period one must keep in mind a context in which young intellectuals were disgusted with the direction in which the country was headed, led mostly by the parents and other relatives of these sophisticated protesters. The renewed vigor of Spanish industry during the late 1950s, especially the tourist industry, after the long and painful lull caused by the civil war, made it easy to put profit and development above solidarity and compassion. The government fostered a stable environment for investments and foreign visitors, clamping down on labor unrest and intellectual dissent. Writers with a social conscience could do little more than paint a vicious portrait of those in power—whether in the family or in larger institutions such as the school, church, or state—often giving remarkably critical reports on their own spiritual nausea, fueled mostly by books, talk, booze, and sex. Marxist vocabulary was in the air, deeply rooted in Spain since the nineteenth century and recycled by union leaders and university students. The divergent foci of Goytisolo's novels discussed in this chapter—the urban poor people and the affluent bourgeoisie—should be considered as a double portrait of a society he understood at the time as deeply divided into social classes: the disorganized and exploited poor; and the rich, lost in a hedonistic frenzy. At best, some of these rich revelers suffer a shallow metaphysical disquiet caused by their consciousness of their parasitic existence. Only intimated in the background of these tales of bourgeois consciences is the fact that some activists risked jail or an even worse destiny—torture or death—in order to change society. Goytisolo, in the tradition of the prophets, demands change by delving into the despair of poverty and the vanity of the rich.

78

El circo, 1957 (The Circus), *Fiestas*, 1958 (*Fiestas*), and *La resaca*, 1958 (The Undertow or The Scum): Exploring the Social Territory

Goytisolo groups these three novels into a trilogy called *El mañana efímero* (The Fleeting Tomorrow). This title echoes the title of a poem by Antonio Machado, "El mañana efímero," in which the poet offers a critical appraisal of Spain and a somber prospect for its future, unless generous ideas and the rage of the oppressed rise to defeat the established order.[1]

I will discuss the trilogy here in the order in which the separate works were released, although *Fiestas* was written in 1955, before *El circo*, the first published. Curiously, Goytisolo has disavowed *El circo* and did not include this novel in his *Obras completas*. This decision is hard to understand at first, because the novel enjoyed several editions and has been translated into Russian and Gaelic. *El circo* consists of 246 pages that are easy and entertaining, two adjectives not often associated with Goytisolo's production. The story line, complex and well handled, with the crispness of a film script, follows the adventures of several characters, bringing them together in a climactic end. A bohemian painter with the exotic name Utah goes from a town at the seaside, Las Caldas, to Madrid, hoping to obtain money from his father, but he is rejected. He returns home in a taxi, and during the long ride, he imagines his lackluster existence is the life of a high-ranking officer in the army or a criminal. He desires power but can attain it only by performing imaginary roles. Meanwhile, in Las Caldas, where the inhabitants are celebrating the town's annual festival, Atila plans a robbery. He is a southern immigrant from Murcia, the tough lower-class man who makes his appearance in only slightly varied versions in many of Goytisolo's novels. Atila seduces a middle-class young woman and an intellectual adolescent, Pablo, who greatly enjoys being dominated by his admired Atila. The Murcian and Pablo assassinate the rich man in town, Don Julio, but it is Utah who claims responsibility for this crime, probably as a substitution for killing his own father.

Homosexuality, sadism, masochism, a violent rebellion against the establishment, the assassination of a paternal figure, the magnification of one's life by appropriating the life of others, all these topics of great importance in Goytisolo's work are handled here with dexterity. But *El circo* is the last of his novels that the censors allowed him to publish in Spain, and he paid a heavy price to remain within the boundaries of the permissible. In an interview, Goytisolo stated that his greatest danger as a young writer was not censorship but self-censorship (Geist 38). *El circo*'s narrative techniques include allusions, suggestions, and implied meanings, as ways of presenting its most valued ideas and criticisms in meaningful but easily overlooked silences. Self-censorship in *El circo* goes beyond the undeveloped figure of an anarchist or the timid denunciation of the unreliability of newspapers. Homosexuality, sadism, and masochism are distanced from the narrator, as if he frowned at these unseemly aspects of his characters. Not until much later, when Goytisolo's father was dead and the son was writing for an international market free from censorship, would he identify with such characters, in a deep exploration of the fascination of violence and an acceptance of homoeroticism.

The title of the novel suggests another reason for Goytisolo's dislike for this novel. On the surface, the circus is a fitting image for several simultaneous happenings, as they occur in a three-ring circus. It also points to the unexamined deceptions and pretenses of the characters. Both Utah and Pablo, the two intellectuals who are closest to the author in social class and education, are guilty of Don Julio's murder only by a voluntary act of identification. Pablo loves Atila and willingly becomes an accomplice; Utah usurps the murderer's aura to compensate for his own lack of significance. Later in his career, Goytisolo would understand that their pretended guilt by association hides a deceptive claim of innocence. Pablo, it would appear, is only guilty of love, Utah of excessive imagination, both venial and even commendable sins. But these intellectuals are guilty in a more radical sense, because, unlike the uneducated Atila, they know they are censoring their own degraded truth, their fascination with power, violence, and destructive barbarism. In a way, they are performing their true selves—or they access their true selves only while performing—believing all the time they are only participating in an entertaining show. They appropriate Atila's crime to hide their own bad consciences and vapid existence.

Fiestas weaves together several stories related only in that they touch the lives of the inhabitants of an apartment building in Barcelona. Pira is a ten-year-old who is living in her uncle's apartment but dreams of escaping to Rome, where she imagines her father works for the pope and awaits her in a castle. Her uncle, Don Paco, once a widower, has retired from his work in the railroads and has several children with his present wife, Doña Cecilia. She has two grown children from a previous marriage. One of them, Arturo, spends most of the time spying with his binoculars out the window. He is disabled, resentful, and afraid of the migrants who have made of the hill facing his apartment a shantytown. Above Don Paco's family lives Enrique, a decrepit man dominated by his wife, a hard-nosed businesswoman. She has recently sold many illuminated crosses to celebrate the event all Barcelona awaits, the World Faith Congress. In another apartment the twelve-year-old Pipo lives with his mother and grandmother. They rent out a room to a teacher, Ortega. Pipo steals money from his grandmother who is senile—an episode Goytisolo reveals in his autobiography as based on his own constant pilfering of his grandmother's purse—and escapes frequently to the harbor to fraternize with a strong sailor called Gorilla. Here again Goytisolo transposes an important event of his youth, when he became infatuated with a sailor who awoke in him, chastely and unacknowledged, his budding homoeroticism.[2] A homosexual neighbor, Benjamín, plans to seduce Pipo but repents at the last minute, gripped by shame and fear. Gorilla confesses to Pipo that years ago he killed a policeman, who had attempted to detain him for making love to a woman on a public beach.

The stories unravel dramatically. Pira, who had hoped she would win the raffle for a tour of Italy, is disappointed and takes off with a one-legged Frenchman who promises to take her to Rome but instead murders her. To make the city more presentable to the many foreign tourists and dignitaries attending the World Faith Congress, the authorities evict the immigrants and raze the shantytown. Pipo gets drunk and reveals Gorilla's secret to a detective who proceeds to arrest the sailor. Ortega, the teacher, is fired. Dressed up as a proper well-to-do boy, Pipo attends the celebrations of the World Faith Congress, his rebellion subdued by his treason, at least for the time being.

Clearly, the story-line of this novel is overheated and emphatic. These topics—slumming, betrayal, exploitation of immigrants—have been treated better by Goytisolo elsewhere. Pipo's adventures and drinking are implausible for a boy his age. Gorilla, whose memories of Africa are unredeemably racist and misogynist, is hardly a compelling character. Arturo, the rabid cripple who is happy only when the immigrants from southern Spain are evicted, is a caricature of the vigilant fascist who is much better developed in Juan Marsé's acclaimed novel *Si te dicen que caí* (1973, *The Fallen*). Pira's murder is a heavy-handed symbol of the space reserved in a repressive society for imagination, originality, and innocence.

Still, there are several memorable sections. Chapter four tells the story of a young man for whom the schoolteacher Ortega has provided contact with an underground leftist group. He agrees to meet this group's representative at a park in the evening, in the same place where Sebastián awaits an unknown homosexual friend. The resulting confusion ends when Sebastián attempts to kiss the young leftist, who runs away calling for the police. In terms of language, homosexuals and underground political groups use an identical register dictated by repression and censorship. Sadly, the leftist in this novel not only rejects Sebastián but essentially joins forces with his enemies to punish him. While the tone here is lighthearted and the story could be misunderstood as a joke at the expense of homosexuals and their secretive ways, the subsequent development of Goytisolo's work tells us to read into this scene the pain and embarrassment of clandestine desire.[3]

The backdrop of the World Faith Congress is effective in providing a collective frenzy that annuls heterodox individuals. The pervasive use of loudspeakers, both by publicity agents of a chocolate factory and by the organizers of the congress, magnifies these voices with an artificial authority. Pira's death and Pipo's treason are offerings to two idols of the modern age: Pira is a victim of her faith in publicity, the lure of the raffle prize and the image of her father which her mother concocted based on a movie; Pipo succumbs to an equivalent authority, and by helping imprison Gorilla, he cordons himself off from the more primitive and, for Goytisolo, more sincere urges of human beings.

La resaca is another attempt to portray the poor and marginalized of Barcelona. Here again, several intersecting story lines lead to treason, abuse of authority, and death. Antonio, the son of a drunkard, is a child who joins a gang of adolescent petty thieves as the apprentice of their leader, Metralla. A woman follows Antonio around the slum because he looks like her only son, who died young. She pays Antonio's parents and brings him home. Other characters include Giner, who was a labor organizer during the republic and now seeks to become active again, despite the bitter opposition of his wife and children. Saturio is the only character who seems to be improving his station in life. He is well connected to the church and has a loving wife, several athletic children, and a brother who works for Coca-Cola and is a champion boxer. He is even in line for an apartment in a better neighborhood. Completing the cast of main characters, there is an old beggar who is a proud veteran of several wars, and Coral, a young prostitute.

As in *Fiestas*, the end here coexists with a communal celebration on the occasion of the World Faith Congress. The contrast of the city's jubilation and the disastrous endings of these stories creates a melodramatic poignancy. To escape to America with Metralla, Antonio steals a large amount of money from the woman who wishes to adopt him, but he is left stranded and betrayed as Metralla disappears with the money. He returns to the woman and becomes her lover, bringing an end to his childhood. Giner cannot galvanize other workers into action and is arrested when he insults the authorities who are evicting the beggar from his home. The beggar, despairing of finding another shelter, commits suicide. Saturio's youngest daughter dies of poisoning when she eats the gunpowder from the fireworks for the night of Saint John, and Saturio becomes so distraught that he drinks heavily, losing the confidence of the priests and the apartment they had promised. Coral is sent to a reformatory. The novel ends when Saturio's son, who has been chosen to read a speech for the inauguration of an urban project, manages to mumble only "We are poor."

How successful is Goytisolo in expressing what Saturio's son cannot? In the first place, the author could not directly reach his Spanish public, because censorship prohibited the publication of the novel, and it had to appear in Paris. Significantly, the only thread of the novel that does not end badly is the story of Emilio, a young worker who has immigrated to France. He has prospered, but decides to return to Spain in the hope of transplanting the social justice he has encountered abroad. His expectations shattered, he returns to France, escaping his country, as Metralla did when he fled to America in search of a better future. But the novel also implies that this neighborhood is a network of multiple voices that can awaken in solidarity if the connections shown by the story are perceived and accepted. The many references to fragmentation—the varied materials used to build the houses, the different origins of the southern immigrants to Barcelona, the buzz of radios, banners, and loudspeakers—are counterbalanced by the ties of friendship, business, and sex that bring everyone together in one communal flow.

Perhaps the most important aspect of these novels is how they convey to readers the dissatisfaction of the writer with the social conditions and the historical moment in which he lives. The lack of greatness he perceives is challenged, as Gonzalo Navajas has pointed out, with an appeal to the noble virtues of human beings, such as magnanimity and solidarity, but also with an idealism that may touch on madness and the sublime. Judged in the context of their time, they are effective, courageous, and valuable novels (Navajas, *La novela* 92). In the development of Goytisolo's work, they include explorations of topics that are frequent parts of his imaginary world: male bonding through violence, sex, and crime; treason; and humiliation as a form of spiritual discipline. While these topics still appear in this trilogy in the context of a traditional evaluation of what is good and evil, they begin to tug at the borders of the narration with a fascination all their own. There is a certain greatness in Metralla, who escapes poverty with a decisive act of treason. Coral's introduction of Antonio to the pleasures of sex has been singled out by Gil Casado as the best part of *La resaca* (*La novela* 373). The violence of Gorilla, Utah, and Metralla acquires a heroic glow that will be explored later in greater depth. While these are still works of apprenticeship, they already show intimations of the master to come.

A collection of short stories published in Buenos Aires in 1960, *Para vivir aquí* (To Live Here), shows a writer stretching to explore new topics. Nevertheless, many materials seem remnants from the previous novels. The first story, "Cara y Cruz" (Heads and Tails), expands on *Fiestas*, describing how prostitutes were removed from Barcelona to Gerona during a religious congress. Here, as in the second story, "Suburbios" (Suburbs, but with a designation that refers, in Spain, to shantytowns), an upper-middle-class narrator observes with indifference the life of his friends, devoted to sex and to having fun. The narrator's experience of not being comfortable in any of the niches society has to offer increasingly becomes the preferred point of view in Goytisolo's writing. Other stories of this collection, "La guardia" (The Watch), "La ronda" (Bar Hopping), "Los amigos" (The Friends), and "Aquí abajo" (Down Here), are all in the form of dour yet sharp observations by up-per-middle-class intellectuals of the life of the lower classes. Taken to-gether, a prisoner who is in jail for borrowing money to play the numbers in the soccer league, a primitive and gifted dancer, a drunkard veteran, and the promiscuous wife of a traveling salesman form in these stories a gallery of victims lost in an indifferent and ruthless society.

The three most developed stories, "Otoño, en el puerto, cuando llovizna" (Autumn, in the Harbor, When it Drizzles), "El viaje" (The Trip), and "Aquí abajo," are characterized by their attention to detail and successful re-creation of deeply felt spaces. In the first story, which takes place at a small bar close to the harbor, a young man, about to leave for Paris, reminisces about all he has learned, especially from his friend Raimundo, a fisherman. While the premise that these workers are more interesting and better than their bourgeois friends is perhaps underlined too heavily, the language of the story revels in the vocabulary of boating and fishing, displaying a fascination with the richness of words familiar to workers of the sea but probably new to most readers of the story. In this stress on the importance of language in defining a living space, Goytisolo is following the path of many earlier writers in Spain, such as José María Pereda (1833–1906), or Cela, but with a more radical pro-gram than either of them. His project here is closely related to the novels of Ignacio Aldecoa (1925–1969), who re-created the lives of Gypsies, civil guards, fishermen, and many other marginal characters in a series of novels and short stories characterized by a rich language adapted to each circumstance. The lyric force of the re-creation of workers' lives also ties these stories to the Italian writer Cesare Pavese (1908–1950), who in turn had been greatly moved by the poetry of Walt Whitman. Goytisolo is never a naive writer, but mobilizes instead, in each text, a tradition he knows well, creating a collective voice that comments at once on the represented world and on literary tradition.

In "El viaje" a couple travels to southern Spain in a pilgrimage for a simpler and more natural life. At first they delight in what they see, lovingly described, but soon they are irritated by the insipid food, provincial gossip, and spying children, who force them to move their nudist bathing further and further from town. This is one more version of Goytisolo's preoccupation with transitional spaces, where characters get stranded when they cannot bear their present situation but are unable to adapt to new circumstances.

"Aquí abajo" is an unusual story for Goytisolo, in that it is the detailed and straightforward account of the life of an intellectual young man, fresh from a two-year stay in Paris, who has joined the army for his military service as an officer. He is skeptical about any possibility of real change in Spanish society and Franco's government. He lands an easy job in an office, gets immensely bored, drinks mightily, frequents prostitutes, and has an affair with a married woman whom he treats cruelly. The officer feels superfluous, his existence unjustifiable. News seeps in of a student revolt in Barcelona, organized by some of his friends. This awakens him to his possibilities of action, and he volunteers to teach a class of the uneducated recruits with whom he connects in a spirit of camaraderie and shared criticism of the authorities. Much of this story has an autobiographical basis, and it is dedicated to his brother Luis Goytisolo, who was actively involved in politics. The daily life in the barracks is vividly re-created, and the character's progressive spiritual nausea is convincing, even if his easy and benevolent relationship with the recruits borders on paternalism and seems more ideal than real. The internal tug of the story, though, is between cynical contemplation and action, and the tipping of the balance toward action bears the typical Goytisolo imprint. The message is clear: to be truly alive each moment, to be a creature of the times, the individual in society must evolve and assume the consequences of responsible action. The inheritance of both existentialism and Marxism weighs heavily on this insistence on the necessity of change for historical and personal reasons.

The next two novels depict the rich and bored. *La isla* (1961, *Island of Women*, also published as *Sands of Torremolinos*) follows the narrator and protagonist, Claudia Estrada, during eleven days in her native Torremolinos, where she returns after many years of absence that included a long stay in Paris. She is married to Rafael, a journalist from neighboring Málaga, who excelled in his career until his alcoholism, philandering, and cynicism caught the eye of his superiors, who sent him back from Paris to Madrid to await a new assignment. Claudia, who during the civil war was engaged in relief operations and full of idealism, has also lost her bearings. Her marriage has come to a dead end, the couple only remaining together to keep a front for Rafael's employers. When Claudia arrives in Torremolinos, the icon of the fun-loving tourist explosion of the late 1950s, she joins a group of idle people who need to fill their time with conversation, alcohol, and sex. Almost everyone is promiscuous, especially an American woman, and they are all unhappily married. Rafael has a French lover, who in turn has an Italian lover. Claudia has a passionate relationship with the editor of a Seville newspaper, but it flounders because he is impotent, perhaps a grimly humorous symbol of the inability of the Spanish press to report the news straight.

The novel delves into the clash of cultures caused in Spain by the tourism industry, which produced, as an unanticipated side effect, the liberalization of sexual mores. The Catholic church's condemnation of bikinis, premarital sex, and divorce could not counter the seductive example of foreigners who seemed happy, wealthy, and respectable, even if they broke every one of these rules, bathing in the nude and indulging in numerous affairs, scandalously even crossing the barriers of social class. Characters choose immediate gratification over the postponed reward of ideals; they prefer the sands of Torremolinos to a promised heaven; and they reduce each other to commodities that circulate feverishly, grabbed for satisfaction and discarded when boredom sets in. Goytisolo's novel does not represent this as a happy situation, but it equally condemns the restrictive sexual practices of the past. He straddles the issue uneasily, noting that for Spaniards who wish to imitate the liberated style of foreigners, the imprint of ancestral ideals lodged indelibly in the superego will produce a feeling of failure, guilt, and pain. Just as the urban development of the town into an international playground is not an unmitigated blessing, the pilgrimages from bed to bed and bar to bar leave bitter memories and hangovers. At the end of the novel, a cat eats a canary and the bloodied feathers serve as a symbol for the loss of innocence of the town and its inhabitants. As Claudia takes off to join Rafael in his new post in New York, she meditates on fleeting time and the unrelenting erosion of her life.

How well does Goytisolo give voice to a woman's thoughts? Claudia, the narrator, does not seem to have a life of her own. Her intellectual pursuits are reduced to attempting to get through Vladimir Nabokov's (1899–1977) *Lolita* (1955), but she manages to read only a few pages at a time. The Russian émigré's novel had first been published in Paris and was a huge success partly for the scandalous nature of the sexual relations it portrays between a mature man and a young girl. In Claudia's hands, therefore, it becomes another icon of her Parisian veneer and openness of mind, but her failure to make much of an inroad into the novel cannot impress readers with her interest in literature. Claudia's admired friend, the actress Dolores Vélez—perhaps not coincidentally, Lolita's full first name is also Dolores—has hardly a thought for her career and spends most of her time agonizing because she is growing older and her husband, Román, is no longer interested in her. But the men in the novel are not more interesting. Insulated from their professional lives in the sanctuary of Torremolinos, their thoughts hardly ever ascend above their waists. They are burnt-out cases wallowing in self-pity. Enrique, the publisher, who manages to express a few sharp lines about the sorry state of Spanish society, is impotent, sarcastic, and has as his right-hand man a dwarf. Readers become voyeurs of a particularly vapid way of life, suggesting that this portrayal is not meant to be imitated. For Goytisolo, no man or woman can remain for long an island to him or herself and prosper in good spiritual health.

The topic of unsatisfactory love relationships is explored in depth in *Fin de fiesta. Tentativas de interpretación de una historia amorosa* (1962, *The Party's Over*). This work contained four long stories connected only in that they are variations on a theme. As Gonzalo Sobejano acutely observes, not only should we consider it a novel but also a model of what is a characteristic form of the novel in the contemporary period. The fragmentation and lack of harmonious unity of the characters' lives are reflected in the isolation of their stories which alludes to the disjointed existence of the city dweller in an industrial society (Sobejano, *Novela* 361–62). The narrator of the first story—each story has no name other than the ordinal number—is an outside observer of a Swedish couple vacationing in a coastal town south of Granada; the husband tells the second story, the wife the third, and a friend of the husband the fourth, in a kaleidoscopic assortment of views. What is notable is that, in all of them, regardless of who tells the story, there is an enigmatic residue, as if passions were ultimately unfathomable. The intentionally barren language of some of Goytisolo's previous novels is replaced here by a highly lyrical and rich vocabulary, evocative and complex, weaving an atmosphere that is dense, credible, and palpable.

In the first story, the narrator is a young boy in a small coastal town who is preparing during the summer for his entrance to a school in Granada. His vision, therefore, is tinged with anticipated nostalgia. A Swedish couple at the main hotel arrives on a bus, attracting everyone's attention. As part of their luggage they carry a sewing machine, which we are informed later the man, a journalist, uses to make lace. The couple spend most of their time arguing and drinking. They rent the boat of the narrator's admired friend Ramón, a muscular young fisherman who has a girlfriend in a neighboring town. The Swedish woman and Ramón make love a couple of times with the knowledge of the husband, who is reviled by her and botches a suicide attempt before they decamp. Why did the couple argue? What was the purpose of their stay? What is the effect of the woman's affair with Ramón—these are questions the narrator is unable to answer. What is clear is the enormous gulf between the behavior of the foreign couple and the traditional mores of the town's inhabitants. They are amazed at the woman's audacity and ashamed of her husband's unmanly behavior. They cannot understand a man who uses a sewing machine, tolerates his wife's having a blatant affair, and allows her to berate him publicly. The fishermen's ideal behavior, which would call for beating or killing the woman, would probably seem to most readers as inappropriate as the dour passivity of the foreign journalist seems to the townspeople. This dysfunctional behavior of human beings implicitly allows a magnified role for the simpler splendor of nature, from the muscular body of Ramón to the daily concerted display of colors and movement by the boats, fish, birds, and sea that the narrator greatly admires.

In the second story, Alvaro, a lawyer, defends the poor and has a brilliant career, but he is feeling old in his early thirties and has lost enthusiasm for his life and marriage. We meet him while he is driving across Barcelona with Loles, an adolescent who fawns over him—Alvaro's Lolita—and idolizes his wife, Ana. He takes Loles to a bar in a seedy part of town, close to the cemetery. There he is a hero and feels useful. He receives the message that a man has been looking for him, but Alvaro is too tied up in his own lamentations to follow up on this inquiry. Later he finds out that the man despaired of meeting him and has left for France without a passport, hoping to sneak through the border. Alvaro, Ana, Loles, and other friends involved in a tempestuous relationship go out to dinner, and Alvaro alienates everyone with his brooding and sulking. Loles walks home but never gets there: she calls Alvaro early the next morning from a bar where she is completely drunk and about to be picked up by a man. Alvaro and Ana intervene and return Loles safely home. Ana leaves for the day on an outing with an admirer and returns to inform Alvaro that she may be in love with another man. The story closes when she discovers a gray hair and Ana and Alvaro lament their deteriorating bodies and life.

The third story begins when the narrator, Marta, gives her husband, Juan, a letter from her lover, Jaime. We are not told why, if as a provocation or an act of trust. Juan becomes depressed, and they escape from Barcelona in the late summer, seeking to restore their bodies and marriage along the coast. They arrive at a small town, south of Alicante, where they are the only guests in the hotel, except for a young Portuguese woman whose family left her there for the summer as punishment. Why, we never know. She seems to have a sentimental relationship with the son of the hotel owner and appears to be taken ill and moved to a hospital. Eventually her parents come to retrieve her, but we get only a glimpse of their car. In the meantime, Juan and Marta go out fishing with Isabelo, one more incarnation of Goytisolo's handsome and rugged fisherman. Juan is jealous, but Marta is faithful to him. Jaime and his wife arrive, and he is outraged when he discovers Marta has told Juan about their affair. They all go to Cartagena to paint the town red, but manage only to bicker among themselves and drink to excess. The next morning, Juan seems reconciled with Marta, returning the letters, and cryptically observing that they now have no importance. Has he concluded that his wife loves him and the affair with Jaime was only a fling? As in the first story, the unruly and mysterious passions of human beings are complemented by nature, in the form of unpredictable weather and a superb atmospheric description of a decrepit summer resort late in the season. The narrator sets a contemplative mood, content to observe the inexplicable without prodding for answers.

The fourth and last story is the most elaborate, drawn out in a strikingly morose and rich language reminiscent of the Italian nobleman Giuseppe di Lampedusa's (1896–1957) *The Leopard* (1958), a story, like this one, about the decadence of aristocracy. In Goytisolo's narration, a young man, Bruno, returns to Spain from five years abroad, during which time he has been teaching Spanish literature at universities in several European cities, among them, as we would expect by now, Paris. He visits the old countryside manor of his friend Miguel and his brother Armando, a place he associates with some of the best years of his life, since he was taken in by Miguel's mother after his father died. But all is not well in the manor. Armando is in jail, for political activities, we assume. Miguel has published a book about the Spanish Erasmists— those open-minded disciples of Erasmus of Rotterdam (c. 1466–1536) whose repression exemplifies for many the intolerance of Spanish decadence—but is depressed and misanthropic. To the despair of his dynamic, intelligent, and witty wife, Mara, he refuses to accept offers to teach at American universities. Bruno is unable to recover the easy friendship he once shared with Miguel, except briefly when they go hunting. He writes to his lover in France, has an affair with a strident woman in Barcelona, and eyes Mara with growing desire.

Other visitors to the mansion include Armando's lover, whose mediocre mind and dramatic suffering drive Miguel to despair. Whether any work is going on to sustain this life devoted to sunbathing, drinking, and soul-searching is not altogether evident. Mara rejects Bruno's advances, Armando is set on the street, and Miguel breaks into tears declaring the party is over. What we have witnessed as readers is more a wake than a party, but in the margins and between the lines there is still the glow of a previous period, a golden age Bruno enjoyed, presided over by a loving mother (with the father and his discipline conveniently removed), and in which all social classes worked in harmony, loving and respecting each other. This aristocratic dream cannot be sustained in the present, and probably only Armando has any inkling of how to adapt to the changing times.

The party was over, and so was this period in Goytisolo's career. With this brooding story, wonderfully textured along traditional narrative lines, he stopped attempting to capture a revolution in soothing and recognizable forms. In the future the economical, social, and moral transformation of Spain would crumble the syntax and shatter the narrative line in his novels, making them some of the most remarkable and original of the second part of the century in Spain.

Notes

1. The relation between the poem and each novel of the trilogy is studied by Ugarte, *Trilogy*. 6–16. More important than the interplay between the poem and the novels, though, is Goytisolo's adoption of a major figure of Spanish letters, Antonio Machado, to inscribe himself within a tradition of rebellion, a strategy that will be developed extensively in later works.

2. This important episode of his youth is narrated in *Forbidden Territory*. It provides the basis of a remarkable story, "Otoño, en el puerto, cuando llovizna" (Autumn, at the harbor, when it drizzles), of his 1960 *Para vivir aquí* (To Live Here) and is slightly transposed in the first episode of *Fin de Fiesta* (*The Party's Over*), which I will discuss later in this chapter.

3. In "Aquí abajo," a story of *Para vivir aquí*, an army officer, after a failed suicide attempt, leaves for the Foreign Legion in order to conquer the passions and shame brought on by homosexual desire. That both *Fiestas* and "Aquí abajo" are ostensibly about other topics, and homosexual desire is only a marginal episode, is itself a form of repression of a topic that, as described in *Forbidden Territory*, was foremost in Goytisolo's mind at the time.

CHAPTER SIX

The Trilogy of Liberation

Bringing Language into Question

 Three novels published within a decade and intimately related to each other form the body of Goytisolo's most significant accomplishment: *Marks of Identity* (1966), *Count Julian* (1970), and *Juan the Landless* (1975). In these novels Goytisolo brings into clear focus topics he had previously explored—family, sex, language, history—now presenting them with increasingly daring departures from the form of the traditional novel, progressively shattering the story line, the coherent portraiture of characters, the pretense of mimesis, and even standard syntax. The operating principle of these radical novels is that revolutionary ideas cannot be couched in terms of nineteenth-century literature, but instead should be incorporated into every aspect of the work. To question profoundly the identity that society imposes on people, the very language of this questioning must be examined. A novel that tells the story of a character, his or her struggle against the world, without challenging readers is similar to the air-conditioned tourist buses Goytisolo abhors and ridicules in several of his novels. They offer the illusion of adventure amid the comforts of home.

Goytisolo demands more. His novels are an unconditional search for *a truthful life*—not for *a truth* that could become institutionalized and be imposed as a dogma on others—and they drive away the reader who is not willing to examine his or her own cherished certainties. Is Spanish civilization worth celebrating? Can heterodoxy be right and orthodoxy wrong? Could chaos be more productive than order? Should one contemplate seriously the possibility of getting off the bus and starting a new life in a different country? Indeed, because of these and other uncomfortable interrogations, these novels tend to produce passionate reactions from readers—some favorable, many negative—a considerable accomplishment at a time when most readers have become jaded by an overload of images and the tendency to observe the world as detached spectators. For those courageous enough to follow Goytisolo in his path through destruction and liberation, for those who will read actively and listen at times to the second-person narrative as if it were addressed to them, these novels offer an experience unmatched in contemporary Spanish letters.

Many of the techniques he uses to elicit an intense reaction from his readers can be found in other works before his, especially by vanguard writers of the early part of the century and the Latin American novelists of the 1960s "Boom." The friendship between Juan Goytisolo and Carlos Fuentes is long-standing, and *Marks of Identity* has many similarities to the Mexican writer's *The Death of Artemio Cruz*, a masterful novel of 1962.[1] The rebellion against inherited roles has been forcefully expressed before, for example by James Joyce in his *A Portrait of the Artist as a Young Man* (1914–1915), and the relativity of social values has been denounced in different but complementary ways by Kierkegaard, Nietzsche, and Marx. It would be, therefore, a mistake to claim that Goytisolo's novels are original—as the Romantics understood this word—and he himself never makes such claims of originality. On the contrary, he affirms precisely the postmodern belief that personality and writing are always constructed from inherited materials, the origins of which are in turn impossible to ascertain. Yet seldom in Spanish letters have novels affected a significant readership with such a refined and forceful combination of daredevil technique, ardent polemical spirit, and profound thought. Goytisolo's uncompromising scrutiny of his tradition and the unmasking of its false pretenses to be universal, eternal, and natural open up a space for life to flow unimpeded by anachronistic ideas and expectations.

Confronting *Marks of Identity*

A photographer, Alvaro Mendiola, who tries to give a satisfactory order to the memories of his life provides the basic structure of *Marks of Identity*. He is a Spaniard, living in Paris, a character that with only slight variations Goytisolo had used before, for example, in the fourth story of *The Party's Over*. During a few days in August 1963 when he is back in Spain, he is allowed to scrutinize his past, delving into his recollections to come to terms with the history of his generation, including events of the civil war. Alvaro also uses a series of photographs and documents as catalyst for remembering history. He discusses these pieces of time with his lover, Dolores (the daughter of a Republican exiled in Mexico), and other friends who show up, not always welcome, at their refuge in Spain for endless drinking and conversation. This frame implies that the past is gone and only images survive, fragmented, modified, mediated, and subject to various interpretations.[2]

The novel opens with a string of quotations in which a composite voice accuses Alvaro of being unpatriotic because of a documentary he had directed exposing poverty in Spain, a film that was ultimately sequestered by the authorities.[3] The composite voice's function is similar to that of the chorus in a Greek tragedy; we become aware that Alvaro is hounded by passionate adversaries who speak as one in the defense of country and religion. They see him as traitorous to his class, ungrateful for all the privileges he enjoys resulting from his education and social standing, and especially monstrous for not upholding the values of his father, who was executed during the civil war by Republican forces for the "crime" of being a representative of the bourgeoisie. It is important to note that these voices are internalized and presented in the text as resounding in the present memory of Alvaro. These voices *inhabit* him. If he has returned to Spain it is not as prodigal son. He is a sort of exorcist, but one who must conjure and expel his own demons.[4] He is urged in this process by a recent heart attack, which has made life's tenuousness evident to him. He wants to balance his account himself, while he is still alive.

The first chapter describes Alvaro's family and childhood. The origin of the family's fortune in the exploitation of black slaves in Cuba haunts him, as the closest example in his own life of the violence and injustice usually hidden by the decorum of civilization. As a child, he finds his life lacking in excitement, except for what can be gleaned from books of the lives of saints and martyrs. Inflamed by his readings, he and his nanny defy the terrors of the civil war raging in the streets and, in search of martyrdom, try to approach a burning church. This anecdote is disquieting: seen from the mature Alvaro's point of view it is a foolish adventure, yet it maintains the aura of a daring action based on firmly held convictions and the example of books. The older Alvaro has become a skeptic but is still nostalgic for existential certainty and literary models.

The chapters of *Marks of Identity* are composed as a musical counterpoint, combining story lines that comment on each other. In the first chapter, the child Alvaro's attempted martyrdom is contrasted to the understated and persevering activities of Jerónimo, an organizer of armed resistance against the dictatorship. Jerónimo works humbly as a laborer at the Mendiolas' country house, sleeping in a stable—a redeemer patterned after Christ, born in a manger—and showing a silent and caring acceptance of young Alvaro's admiring friendship. There is a similar situation in Carlos Fuentes's *The Good Conscience* (1959), in which a boy befriends a runaway rebel but is unable to protect him from being discovered. There, too, the boy is imbued with a religious language of sacrifice and generosity, but eventually he learns his society's lesson, to disassociate his professed ideals from his acts, with the practical aim of preserving his own interests and those of his social class. In Goytisolo's version of a boy's eye-opening encounter with a representative of the fight for social justice, the rebel gets away and the boy eventually follows in his footsteps, using his art—photography and filmmaking—in the service of the oppressed and against the bourgeoisie that bred him. A third strand brings the importance of both religious and political heroism into question: the boy visits his aging grandmother, who does not recognize him. This event—based on an autobiographical experience of the author—reveals to him that nothing is definitive, because time brings about, sooner or later, a haphazard erasure of memory. For Alvaro, the silver lining of this discovery is that he is not wed to his present identity forever. His grandmother releases him, by forgetting who he is, from the obligation of behaving according to the roles imposed on him by a myriad of aleatory circumstances.

The second chapter covers the years when Alvaro was a university student. Here again, an encounter proves decisive. He becomes a friend of Sergio, a rich, frequently drunk, and always rebellious young man who is enrolled at the university but hardly ever goes beyond the cafeteria, preferring to explore the seedy neighborhoods of Barcelona. Becoming Sergio's fervent disciple, Alvaro scuttles his career and discovers a society that is an alternative to the well-to-do middle class of his origins. In embracing his new friends, who are despised and feared by his family, he acts to break away from his past and the future for which this past prepares him. But this traditional story of adolescent rebellion is carefully balanced by two other stories in this chapter.

Sergio's story is complex. His mother is apparently progressive and encourages her son's defiant life, but she is crushed when Sergio finds a permanent lover and withdraws his confidence from her. Later, Sergio marries a socialite and conforms to the life expected from a prominent member of affluent society. His rebellion was skin-deep, more a reaction to an incestuous relationship—a local neurosis—than to the conditions and requirements of his society at large. Without Sergio, though, Alvaro would probably not have found the courage to explore the alternative life that would so radically change him. Sergio is the teacher who points the way toward rebellion, but he lacks the courage to renounce completely the comforts of home. He serves as a reminder that backsliding is always possible, that the position of the rebel is never firmly established but must always be reinvented in the face of an accommodating society that co-opts all forms of resistance and transforms them into spectacle and merchandise. In later books, Goytisolo often expresses the desire to acquire a terrible stigma, be it physical or moral, which would permanently put one beyond recovery by the normal standards of society. This desire that can never be fulfilled—society will always find a way to transform even monstrosity into a money-making proposition—betrays the anxiety caused by figures such as Sergio who, having fallen short of their adolescent ideals and having tired of living on the margin, return to the comfortable fold.

The second story line that complements Alvaro's remembrance of his university years is the fond recollection of one professor, Ayuso, who provided his students with a model of integrity and courage. Imprisoned after the war, forced into exile, he returned to disseminate his message that Spanish history is not a single thread leading to Franco, but rather a complicated interplay of institutions grounded in medieval Spain. A photograph of Américo Castro (1885–1972), dedicated to Ayuso, presides over the professor's living room, indicating he probably taught, as

Castro did during his tenure at Princeton University, that the confluence of Christians, Jews, and Moors had constituted the richest hour of Spanish history.[5]

But chapter one ends with the news of Ayuso's death, and the second chapter places Alvaro's attendance at Ayuso's funeral in the fictive present of the narration. The impression of seeing the unmarked graves of major figures of the Spanish Republic, meticulously described by Goytisolo, leads Alvaro to the conclusion that his teacher's death before he could see a return to democracy proves the failure of his noble resistance and that of his disciples. The hopes of a generation are buried with him under the vigilant eyes of the secret police. Confirming the spirit of failure that pervades this chapter—his two teachers, Sergio and Ayuso, die—the text incorporates the description of the unsuccessful efforts of university students to organize a general strike. Not only is this chapter moving, but it also offers an important clue to the function that Alvaro— and by extension in this case, Goytisolo—attributes to memory. The unmarked graves, the ignored strike, the vanished youth—all show the power of a repressive social system intent on distorting and erasing the past. In opposition, the novel works as a memory machine, performing a revolutionary act by fighting oblivion, incorporating the eulogy for Ayuso which had been forbidden by the police at his funeral. In the context of this chapter, this eulogy transcends its occasion and becomes a eulogy for all the courageous people who were engaged at the time in the struggle for freedom of inquiry and expression.[6]

The third chapter shows Alvaro trying to reconstruct the scene of two violent events: the death of his father, summarily executed with four other men by Republican soldiers during the civil war, and the death of eighteen peasants shot by the civil guard near Yecla in May 1936. One of these episodes, his father's death, is easily accessible: there is a modest monument marking the spot, and his family has kept alive the memory of the suffering occasioned by his disappearance and the belated news of his death. In stark contrast, the peasants' deaths, during a peaceful protest in response to harsh economic conditions and blatant abuse by the town's authorities, have been almost completely forgotten. National memory is as selective as that of any individual: it highlights and cherishes the positive and censors the most negative and damaging. But these episodes, which for different reasons cannot be fully remembered, fester nevertheless in the subconscious and must be brought to light. Until this past is regained, Alvaro, or Goytisolo, cannot simply walk away and leave Spain behind. Alvaro wishes to restore the real in all its fullness, but he encounters an unwilling Spain reticent to examine the origins of her present power structure.

Alvaro moves in the next chapters to examine his ten years of life in exile, which represents a very different experience from that of his friends who stayed in Spain. In Paris, Alvaro is received warmly by leftist intellectuals who promise him support but then brush him off, moving on to representatives of more-fashionable causes. He falls into a subculture of Spanish exiles who endlessly continue the same polemics that divided them at home. The only positive experience is his meeting Dolores and becoming her lover, but this relationship is marred by the growing awareness of his desire for other men—a still-closeted desire that is not yet completely integrated in his life—briefly and elliptically alluded to in Alvaro's anonymous and fleeting sexual encounter with an Arab in Paris.[7] A trip to Geneva, where one of Alvaro's uncles had committed suicide years earlier and where now Dolores has an abortion, confirms Alvaro's pessimism; he does not wish to bring children into a world which for him is marked mostly by suffering. Oddly enough, the couple take along with them Dolores's nephew, perhaps serving as an awkward confirmation that regardless of what they decide about having children, life will perpetuate itself.

In the obligatory counterpoint called for by the structure of this novel, the reader encounters the story of Antonio, Alvaro's friend and collaborator in his frustrated documentary about Spain. Released from prison, where he had been sent after being implicated in subversive activities, he returns to the Andalusian coast, on parole and with his movements restricted to the limits of his hometown. He is shaken by the unremitting poverty of the fishermen and the arrogance of the authorities. The only change he observes is a slight improvement in economic conditions brought about by tourists; an old friend, for example, has a garage and makes a living. If this can be called progress, it has come without the help of Antonio's work in the political underground. Both Alvaro's efforts in Paris and Antonio's meaningless rebellion in Spain speak of a wasted generation. Again, yet a third thread provides a deeper perspective. Alvaro's and Antonio's stories are interrupted by several documents set apart from the rest of the text by italics: they are the excruciatingly detailed secret-police reports concerning the activities that led to Antonio's arrest. These reports have an almost whimsical character, because the agents use inventive nicknames to identify temporarily the people they shadow, but the effectiveness of their methods and the pervasive invasion of privacy they entail make it clear why Alvaro and Antonio are correct in opposing them. Their ultimate success lies not in a triumphant overthrow of the dictatorship, but in retaining a compassionate and independent language to confront the chilling and reductive control of a police state.[8]

In the last chapters, two paths open to liberation. Contrasting specifically with the surveillance reports, a new set of texts in italics represents the recollections of a worker who tries to improve his condition by going to France. He does not receive the job that had been promised to him, his son dies, and he is imprisoned when he returns home and creates a scandal at a public office because the authorities do not take seriously his request to obtain a job. Goytisolo conveys here a quiet desperation with a combination of directness and the reiterated symbol of a chair to which the worker refers in an incantatory way, as a place where only he and those he approves of can sit. This domestic and minimal space, nevertheless, concentrates all the dignity of a life that refuses to give up. In contrast with the longer-winded musings of his intellectual champions, Alvaro and Antonio, this worker, José Bernabeu, packs such sentiment and resilience into his condensed lines that the ultimate failure of the repressive system seems somehow probable.

The narrator breaks away from the regular sentence structure and moves into a series of brief paragraphs and single lines that approach a poetic text and echo the book of Psalms. In the last chapter, Alvaro is observing Barcelona through a telescope, on a hill overlooking the city, and a whirlwind of voices and memories overwhelms him until he realizes his destiny has been fortunate. His destiny has separated him from his family and city, allowing him to love men and women, making him one with the pariahs, associating him with his black relatives, and condemning him to a radical exile he can now cultivate and glorify. Having had the courage to examine in detail the signs of identity stored in his memory, he is able to reject them and embrace his newly found solitude of splendid negativity.

In the final chapters of *Marks of Identity*, language breaks the restrictions of ordinary novelistic prose, abandoning capital letters at the start of sentences and any form of punctuation, grafting into the novel the freedom of contemporary poetry and the incantatory power of ceremonial and collective chant. From this point on, Goytisolo's texts acquire the rhythm of the oral tradition and, as he has often remarked, are better understood when read aloud. More than witnessing events through the description of a historian, this new mode of writing gives readers the impression of overhearing the flow of ideas, images, and emotions of a learned mind, where layers of ancestral culture and hundreds of voices compete for attention. This self is not unified but often splintered and divided into antagonistic factions, many of them nasty, pugnacious, politically incorrect. Present and past coexist simultaneously in this memory theater, and pull the narrating voice in different directions to the point where the continuity of identity becomes a curse.

Count Julian's Creative Revenge

Although the narrator of *Count Julian* remains unnamed, he is in many ways similar to Alvaro Mendiola of *Marks of Identity*. *Count Julian* describes one day in the life of a man who is deeply concerned with and affected by his boyhood, when his mind was colonized by dishonest myths about Spanish history and his body harnessed by guilt. Living alone in Tangier, from where he can see the coast of Spain on the horizon, he reminisces about the past, puts his tradition through a thresher of impassioned criticism, and dreams of leading an invasion of his country, like the one that originated from northern Africa in the year 711.

In one version of Spanish history, an essential austerity of spirit, endurance of the body, and seriousness of mind—mostly male minds—goes back to the origins of human life in the Iberian peninsula. The cave dwellers of Altamira, who painted dashingly spirited horses between 15,000 and 10,000 B.C.; the heroic Celtiberian defenders of Numantia, who resisted the Romans from 195 to 133 B.C., when four thousand of them surrendered to sixty thousand Roman troops who had blockaded the city for six months; Romans such as the Stoic philosopher Lucius Annaeus Seneca (c. 4 B.C.–A.D. 65), born in Cordoba, and the emperor Trajan (53–117, emperor 98–117), also born in Spain; the Visigoths, who established their capital in Toledo in the sixth century and could boast of sophisticated jurists, erudite intellectuals such as Isidor of Seville (c. 560–636), and some of the finest jewelry in Europe—all of them constituted a chosen tradition of ancestors who evinced the essential virtues of the Spanish spirit, culminating in the late fifteenth century with the reign of the Catholic kings: Ferdinand II (1452–1516), king of Aragon, and Isabella I (1451–1504), queen of Castile. Under the reign of Ferdinand and Isabella, Spain became unified, and they defined an official image for centuries to come.

In 1478 the Spanish Inquisition was founded, and it would labor to assure the unity of religious belief. The year 1492 saw the defeat of the last Moorish kingdom in Spain, the fabled Granada. Also in 1492 about 170,000 Jews, many of whom had played a decisive role in the politics, culture, and finances of the several peninsular kingdoms united by the Catholic kings, were summarily expelled. In the same fateful year, the publication of a Castilian grammar by Antonio de Nebrija (c. 1444–c. 1522), the first grammar of a modern vernacular language, made Castilian the language of the empire which would emerge from Columbus's discovery. A few years later, in 1502, the Moors remaining in Spain were given the choice of conversion or expulsion from their homeland of eight centuries. To this account of a process of endurance of a pristine self endangered by successive enemies—Jews, Moors, Protestants—many intellectuals added, and found positive, Spain's resistance to modernization and to the industrial revolution with its sequel of materialism, and to international ideologies such as anarchism and Marxism. Gen. Francisco Franco's crusade in defense of church and country was directly rooted in this heroic line begun in Altamira.

The Moorish invasion represented the greatest deviation from the straight ancestral line, the deepest perversion. The Visigoth domination had crumbled after the death of Witiza in 709, when Rodrigo of Cordoba took over. At the same time, the Moorish expansion, sixty years after the death of the prophet Muhammed (570–632), was in full swing. In 710 at

Ceuta, a city port in northern Africa, only fourteen miles from Spain's shores, the governor, a Christian Moor called variously Ulyan, Julián, Urbano, Ulbán, or Bulián (all names used by Goytisolo in *Count Julian*) entered into an alliance with Muza, the new governor of Muslim Africa. Together they planned the invasion of Spain—some say with the pretext of restoring power to Witiza's family—sending off to the opposing shore Tarik-ben-Zeyad, the governor of Tangier, with seven thousand soldiers who reinforced themselves on a hill called today, in his honor, Gibraltar (Mount Tarik). After the battle of Guadalete in July 711, where Rodrigo's forces were routed by the allied troops of Julián, Tarik, and Muza, the Africans rapidly proceeded to invade most of the peninsula. These events generated the legend that Florinda, the daughter of Count Julian, had been raped by Witiza or Rodrigo.[9] Julián's treason was the result of his moral outrage for a private act. Florinda, as Helen of Troy before her, because of her provocative behavior—why else, so the legend assumes, would Rodrigo have raped her?—was guilty of sending thousands of men to the battlefields. She, of course, is the temptress and Rodrigo merely the victim of his manly passions. Julián is the traitor, Rodrigo a libertine who is punished by being forced to dwell in a pit where he, as a modern Prometheus, is continuously eaten by snakes. Thus was the Christian paradise in Spain lost to the Arabs.[10] It was regained by a woman, Queen Isabella, and the Catholic church's condemnation of the pleasures of the body. Austerity, chastity, loyalty, and unity—these are the virtues that redeemed Spain.

Not for Goytisolo. In this novel, *The Revindication of Count Julian*—to translate the whole Spanish title—or his defense and exoneration, Goytisolo advances an alternative version of Spanish history, one that celebrates excess, treason, sex, and fragmentation. Unless one understands that this text is a response to the previously described interpretation of the collective past, an interpretation that excluded Moors, Jews, and the heterodox, an interpretation imposed upon the people for centuries by the power of the army, the church, and the state, some of Goytisolo's passionate writing may seem unjustified. Readers who have experienced the effects of arbitrary views sustained as a dogma will have an easier time establishing an emotional link with the implied author of this book. One cannot overestimate the importance of homosexual desire as a pivotal instance among the repressed differences in the Spanish society in which Goytisolo grew up. A pervasive condemnation of homoeroticism, often accompanied with verbal or physical abuse, treated a natural form of love as a perversion and condemned homosexual men and women, many of whom had contributed significantly to Spanish culture—it may suffice to mention two great poets of this century, Federico García Lorca (1899–1936) and Luis Cernuda (1902–1963)—to open derision or a life of duplicity and occultation. Therefore, the relationship in *Count Julian* between a corrosive attack against the official version of Hispanic tradition and what amounts to a celebration of the phallus is not at all strained.[11]

In spite of its appearance as an unconstrained flow of thoughts connected only by colons, *Count Julian* is rigorously structured. It is divided into four chapters. The first one is the closest to a traditional narrative and follows the unnamed character from the moment he wakes up in the morning, through his wanderings in Tangier. First he collects dead flies in his kitchen; then he has breakfast at a café, gets a shot of penicillin at a pharmacy to combat his syphilis, proceeds to a neighborhood library where he smashes the dead flies he brought with him between the pages of the Spanish classics, walks through the open market, sits at a café to have a cup of tea, sees the James Bond movie *Thunderball,* and goes into the public baths. During his walk, he meets several people, among them Don Alvaro Peranzules—a Spanish chauvinist—a young boy (who turns out to be his younger self), and a group of tourists. The trivial nature of these pursuits is countered by a commentary that stems mostly from a voice addressing the main character as "you," an aspect of a personality in constant and often polemical dialogue with itself.[12] One of the tourists, nicknamed variously Mrs. Potiphar (a reference to Joseph's temptress in Genesis 39) and the Daughter of the American Revolution, poses for a photograph in the market with a snake around her neck. The snake, in the irritated imagination of the narrator, bites her face and kills her. A group of children gather around her and urinate on her genitals. With this, the introduction of the main themes of this text is complete, and the three other chapters transform, expand, and modulate them.

In the second chapter, the narrator, drowsy from having smoked a pipeful of marijuana, watches a series of television programs from Spain, to which he had included a guide in the first chapter. In the third, he imagines several destructive actions against his fatherland, among them a degrading visit to a Disneyland-like attraction featuring a visit to a large model of Isabella the Catholic's vagina, a brutal invasion of Moorish warriors, and, in some of the funniest pages Goytisolo has ever written, the subtraction of all words of Arab origin from Spanish. The final chapter describes the rape and suicide of his alter ego as a child in Barcelona. The ideal way to read this book is as if it were a dramatic musical composition, similar to jazz variations, such as the "sheets of sound" of John Coltrane's tenor saxophone or Wagner's lavishly textured operas based on a few easily recognizable motifs.

This is a day in the life, but especially in the mind, of an exile. He is still occupied with Spain, and he generates incessant connections between what he has in front of his eyes and memories of his Spanish past, while he indulges in elaborate fantasies of his future relation with his country.[13] Like a spurned lover, but one who has discovered the unworthiness of his beloved, he struggles to break loose from this signifying mechanism that ties him to the past. First of all he must struggle with language in its most evident form, as a series of texts that are handed down from generation to generation as worthy of conservation and representing the best the country can offer. The narrator's raid against the books in the library is an act of desecration, a ritual attack against the aura surrounding Golden Age drama (Calderón, Tirso, and Lope de Vega are especially singled out), the Generation of 98, and the sonnet.[14] The narrator reacts less against the texts themselves than against their canonization by critics, which generates a division between these texts and others. If a reader is repelled by the honor code of the seventeenth century, with its insistence on purity of Christian ancestry, resents Castilian imperialism, does not participate in a set of values that estimates Catholicism, heterosexuality, and conservatism as absolutely superior to other religions, sexual inclinations, or political choices, such a reader is placed in the position not of having different values and critical judgment but of being unpatriotic.

In opposition to this reductivism, *Count Julian* proposes two strategies: satire and celebration. A stream of samples interwoven seamlessly in the text shows the inanity of some of this revered literature, with its exaltation of bloody revenge for marital infidelity and of victorious battles, its enraptured descriptions of arid landscapes, and even its glorification of mountain goats. In some cases, familiar texts are put to radically different uses. For example, a poem by Manuel Machado (1874–1947), "Castilla," describes the Cid leaving for exile with twelve of his followers. He stops for rest and water at a house, but a young girl comes out and begs him to leave, because the king will punish anyone who helps him. A Christlike figure, the Cid keeps on riding, blinded by the sun and stoically enduring thirst and exhaustion. Goytisolo uses these verses, which describe the Cid, a hero who expanded the Christian domain at the expense of Moorish kingdoms, to herald the return of the Moors, led again by Julián, in the reconquest of Spain. Here are the two texts, first Machado's, then Goytisolo's:

El ciego sol, la sed y la fatiga.
Por la terrible estepa castellana,
al destierro, con doce de los suyos
—polvo, sudor y hierro—, el Cid cabalga. (*Antología* 83)
(The blinding sun, thirst, and fatigue.
Through the relentless Castilian steppe,
to his exile, with twelve of his men,
—dust, sweat, and iron—the Cid rides on.)

el ciego sol, la sed y la fatiga! : por la terrible estepa castellana, al descanso, con cientos de los suyos, polvo, sudor y hierro, Ulyan cabalga (260)
(the blinding sun, thirst, and fatigue!: through the relentless Castilian steppe, to his rest, with hundreds of his men, dust, sweat, and iron, Ulyan rides on.)

The celebratory move consists of highlighting a poet, Luis de Góngora (1561–1627), who remained for the most part unpublished during his life, was derided by Lope, and was rescued only in the twentieth century. Góngora is a poet of complexity, sharp wit, extreme erudition, and Latinate syntax, who is concerned more with beauty than morality. The fact that his verses were considered unnatural, unproductive, and pagan

106

allies them with the homosexual activities of the narrator, who has been similarly classified by his compatriots. Góngora's daring reordering of language serves as a model of an individual's potential for freedom and experimentation, even within a strongly established system.

The narrator identifies some of the voices he incorporates into the text while leaving others unmarked and clandestine. For example, at the beginning of chapter two, the narrator compares himself to someone lost in a house of mirrors while spectators outside laugh at him. This is an apposite comparison with the narrator's effort to rid himself of the distorted and interiorized images of himself that he has accumulated during a lifetime. But it also alludes to a moving episode in Jean Genet's *The Thief's Journal*, when Stilitano, the strongman Jean adores, is visibly at a loss in the labyrinth of the Palace of Mirrors (265–66). By invoking Stilitano, Goytisolo inserts in the text an allusion to a writer admired elsewhere but completely beyond the pale of canonical Spanish literature.

Here one could also include another motif, the James Bond movie *Thunderball* that provides many images that are recycled later. The choice, as an important building block for his novel, of what could be considered an object of commercial entertainment originating in a popular form of literature is nothing new and echoes Cervantes's use of novels of chivalry to structure his *Don Quixote*. The narrator of *Count Julian* imitates the British secret agent and, like 007, has a license to kill, but instead of being at the service of a decadent imperial power allied with one superpower against another, he leads third world warriors in the invasion of Europe. From *Thunderball* Goytisolo takes images of the sensuous dance at a carnival in Brazil and of an underwater expedition, transforming the latter scene into a visit to the Turkish baths (interlacing this episode with references to Aeneas's descent into Hades in Virgil's *Aeneid*) and the former into a sensuous dance performed by Queen Isabella. The lack of respect for contextuality and the easy transference of images and irreverent contamination of sacred icons are part of the narrator's program to break free from the shackles of a rigid tradition.

A penicillin shot against syphilis opens two lines of variations. First, the narrator's infection serves as a convenient emblem of his being branded by society as unhealthy because of his sexual proclivities. He

107

dreams of passing on to others this infection, which he refers to as rabies, by donating blood in Spain. His younger self, later in the novel, also experiences the ravages of syphilis. The penicillin shot also triggers the narrator's memory of a demonstration he was forced to witness as a child during a science class, in which a scorpion killed a grasshopper trapped in a glass jar. The needle breaking into his skin and the scorpion's sting paralyzing the grasshopper both serve as images of anal penetration, which, as the novel progresses, acquires the fascination of a transgressive action that simultaneously produces pleasure and pain, both healing and killing.

Don Alvaro Peranzules, the Spanish chauvinist, reappears under many guises, for example, as a teacher and as the Ubiquitous or Ever-present, a reference to General Franco. Similarly, the American tourist, alias Mrs. Potiphar, is blended into the image of Queen Isabella, as well as that of the mother of the philosopher Seneca and Franco, and of the narrator's younger self, Alvarito. These transferences, used in place of distinct characters typical of traditional novels, point out the fact that personalities become interchangeable when they are mass-produced by a powerful societal system. The narrator is keenly aware that his own self is constructed from public materials, much as each sentence we articulate is made of words previously defined by tradition and society. Others are similarly constructed, and he relishes debunking the romantic myth of independent individuals. In this conception of the self as a sentence—a sentenced self, in more than one way—one finds the imprint of Goytisolo's interest in linguistics, a discipline he enjoyed studying for years, and connections to Jacques Lacan's concept of the subconscious (though the latter probably does not indicate a direct influence so much as an affinity with ideas that were amply shared among Parisian intellectuals).

The young boy whom the narrator meets in the first chapter and who serves briefly as an extremely inefficient guide, a boy who reminds the narrator of himself as a child, reappears as one of the protagonists of the closing chapter. By now, the narrator, having disposed of his animosity against his culture and country, is ready to confront the child who still survives in him as a model of habitual good behavior. The boy is associated with Little Red Riding Hood, and the wolf in this story is a Moorish night guard at a construction site in Barcelona. Led by his curiosity about this man's sexual prowess, which has created a scandal in the otherwise quiet neighborhood, the boy goes to his home and soon becomes mesmerized by the man's phallus, returning often to be raped, beaten, and infected with syphilis, eventually being coerced to steal from his family. When urged to bring his mother so that she too can be abused—a Sadean dream—the boy hangs himself.

Sadomasochistic and cross-generational sexual activities such as these remain at the outer fringes of sexual activity and are condemned by most societies.[15] This is, of course, precisely why they are inflicted on the child and the reader, for their revulsive effect. Goytisolo does not offer an alternative most of us can embrace—especially women readers—but a confrontation of two forms of violence that do not even cancel each other. A dogmatic and reductive tradition of mostly male voices is parodied and challenged by disreputable and marginalized expressions of male violence. Goytisolo does not create a new orthodoxy, but offers instead a clash of powerful images that are subjacent in the ordering of society.[16] They are, therefore, not simply images for Freudian or Jungian analysis, but graphic representations of the complex relations of abusive power between human beings. It could be credibly argued that the exploitation by white Europeans of the Moors—treated as if they were animals, wolves—while disguised in the form of constructive colonization, was similarly destructive and brutal, often evoking nevertheless the fascinated complicity of the victim. Therefore, the child is receiving a displaced revenge for the abuses his family and country inflicted on the black slaves in Cuba and the Moors in Spain and Africa. In this sense, he is the expiatory innocent victim that can restore order and bring about conciliation. One can find here a version of one of the West's master plots, our ancestors' expulsion from Paradise for sin and the redemption by means of Christ's sacrifice. This interpretation gives new meaning to the snake which slithers its way throughout the text, from the open market in Tangier to the construction site in Barcelona. Killing Mrs. Potiphar, accompanying the Moorish invaders of Spain, raping the boy, it invites the reader to taste again the feared fruit from the tree of knowledge of

Good and Evil. After listening to this textual snake, we as readers may discover ourselves exposed and naked, expelled from whatever paradise had made us secure.

Juan the Landless, a Textual Adventure

While the three novels of the trilogy are independent, a reader who has read the first two will be better prepared to appreciate *Juan the Landless*. In a sense, these three texts offer a progressive difficulty which teaches active reading. The first of these novels, *Marks of Identity* presents a story line that combines different characters, places, and times with the fluidity of cinematic montage. It still simulates a real world and intimates at times that the implied author has inched closer to the historical truth than the historian. Only in the final pages does the prose become fragmented lyricism, logic receding before the freedom of subjectivity and emotion.

Count Julian traces the outline of an exterior activity—wanderings of an exile in Tanger during one representative day—and then goes inward into the exploration of the clusters of memories, emotions, and fantasies that occupy the narrator. In *Juan the Landless*, very little action is left in a traditional form: the writer is in his house, probably in Paris, mostly in the kitchen, writing. He looks at a record jacket with the photograph of a voluptuous woman on it and some postcards of Cuba, black slaves crouching to defecate simultaneously into an open trench. He picks up his books. He glances at a letter he knows by heart, a respectful request for help from one of his great-grandfather's slaves, a woman abandoned to destitution and separated from her own family after serving her owner's family for years. The letter closes with greetings to the wife and children, each name remembered with poignant fidelity. That is all that happens: we observe a writer at work.[17] But the seven chapters of the book, each one structured differently, are seven entries into the mind of this writer, who happens to be remarkably similar to Juan Goytisolo—an outrageous, imaginative, and sophisticated person. The novel resembles a series of essays or, better still, a tumultuous rush of insights such as precedes the ordered exposition of ideas. There are no footnotes here to buttress the author's authority, no subtle transitions to lead readers into well-rounded conclusions, no humanistic claim for universal validity. These are raw opinions, deeply felt passions, vividly conveyed with a shorthand that is daring and effective.

The first chapter is divided into seventeen sections and begins in the middle of a stream of conscience. The narrator is occupied with thoughts about the denial of the body in high Western culture. He imagines two situations to illustrate this occultation. First, he contrasts the public defecation of slaves into an open trench with the private and secretive use of a toilet by the masters. This apparatus, which is seen here as one extension of the British Empire's strategies of domination, sets apart owner and slave with an artificial value system that in turn is naturalized and generates a myth. It is natural—ideology holds—to hide the "lower" functions of the body. Control of the urge to defecate in order to reserve it to a secretive place and an appropriate time is a requirement for inclusion into society, portending all other deferrals and self-restraints, both physical and spiritual, that the individual will learn during his or her life. Those who do not attain this control are considered barbarous and inferior. With a twisted logic, previous denial is held to be proof of the non-existence of repressed parts of existence: there is no evidence, textual or otherwise, that Christ, the Virgin, or the saints excreted, and therefore they never did. Instead, as Saint Bernard claims, they emanated a pleasant perfume. Alvarito, the narrator's younger self, tries to emulate these models by resisting his urge to defecate, and he finally succeeds, to the jubilation of the heavenly powers.

As Goytisolo makes clear later in the novel, this denial of the full reality of the body, its needs, functions, and desires, has been especially strong in Spain, producing what he calls a constipated culture. Excrement is here, though, not the main repressed element—since Spanish literature has had its fair share of eschatological writing—but it represents all that is denied by polite discourse. Everyone has an anus, and this hidden part of the body, as opposed to the face and the phallus or vagina, has no differentiating function. On the contrary, it generates anxiety about the erasure of important distinctions which define social identity. The feces leaving the body are an intimation of death—the ultimate equalizer—and the anus invokes fears of penetration that threaten the stereotypical distinction between the male as strong, active, and penetrating and the female as weak, passive, and accepting.[18] This is why the buttocks become the emblem of the egalitarian society that the narrator proposes as a utopia later in the novel.

Similarly, in his second imagined scene in the first chapter, another force overpowers the barriers set to restrain it: sex. In the plantation the slaves are kept apart, but during the night they find ways to circumvent all obstacles and gather in boisterous couplings. The priest Vosk preaches to them in vain the benefits of chastity, suffering, endurance, and humility. Instead of waiting to be purified like gold or sugar in the slow fire of their work, they give themselves to the sensuous enjoyment of the present. The plantation owner is shown as God the Father, too lazy to inspect his people himself, so he relies on reports from the White Virgin. She, in turn, gets her information from Vosk, who veils the number, nature, and variety of the couplings he observes by switching to Latin. The Virgin distracts the Father by reciting French poems. Whether anything at all is happening in the slaves' barracks—it may all be the feverish imagination of Vosk and the White Virgin, acting out their own fantasies and stereotypes—the goings-on remain unexamined, displaced and repressed under layers of civility. The narrator wonders how he could become a redeemer of these black slaves? He has to be born again, from the coupling of two Afro-American gods, Changó and Yemayá, canceling and replacing his Christian origins. But how could he? He remains unavoidably white.

Yet white/black is not the only opposition for which he can choose to be on the side of the dispossessed, and in other cases he can be more successful in following through on his inclinations. The rest of the novel explores four realms in which such redeeming choices are possible by contesting the limitations of sex, the space of geography, the narrative of history, and literary tradition. In embracing homosexuality and the Arab word, and in aligning himself with renegades from Europe and critics of realism, the narrator of *Juan the Landless* becomes detestable to established society. As a pariah and a nomad, he does not have to live up to any rules, remain decent, or fulfill obligations. He can acknowledge without any shame all his feelings and desires. He does not need to hide his body. He can forsake his language.

Sexual activity is considered absolutely legitimate, even necessary and commendable, when it is restricted to a young heterosexual, married couple, as long as it occurs in private and with the purpose of procreation. All deviations from this pattern have attracted, and still attract, some level of condemnation from considerable sectors of society. Even "legitimate" sex has been considered only second best to absolute celibacy by Christianity. A partial listing of activities that deviate from the alleged ideal will test the limits of any reader's tolerance: masturbation; premarital sex; monogamous lesbian relationships; monogamous male homosexual relationships; interracial sex; adultery; female and male homosexual promiscuity; group sex; exhibitionism; sex with old, sick, ugly, and dirty people; sadomasochism; fetishism; transvestism; sex for money; incest; pedophilia; necrophilia. The purpose of this list is to show that although most of us will draw the line at some point, our limits are not "natural." Certain activities which are allowed in some societies and at some times are forbidden in other times and places. Interracial marriages can be unremarkable in some countries, a crime in others. Sex between a professor and a student is today in America the most frequent ground for dismissal from a tenured position. What goes in New York or Barcelona is not always acceptable in St. Louis or Oviedo. A waiter may openly lead a life that would get a manager fired.

The arbitrary nature of these rules that define what is permissible in sex and the virulence with which they are applied are flouted and parodied in the second chapter of *Juan the Landless*. It opens with the narrator making love in the marketplace with an aged beggar, who would appear repugnant to most people. The catalyst of this chapter seems to be an insensitive remark that has infuriated the narrator, when a Spanish woman asks her elegant husband to stand aside so that he is not touched by a passing beggar. The narrator counters with an action that generates the awe, fascination, and condemnation of an assorted group of international tourists. The narrator is not naive, and observes that while he and his partner in breaching the rules of common decency are condemned, the cameras record the scene which will circulate back home as a monstrous confirmation of the need for surveillance, control, and punishment. The power of conventions runs deep, and a single act of defiance does not undermine it. Therefore, the narrator turns against the "cute reproductive couple" that is praised by all countries and elevated into a myth by the machinery of publicity. This beautiful young couple everywhere reminds those who are not like them that they are inferior. Against this couple, whom he presents attempting to make love publicly at Bloomingdale's with the store's blessing, he raises the specter of King Kong, of alligators roaming the sewers of Manhattan, of dangerous snakes lurking in parks, of transvestites, and of a different race, the Arabs.[19] What matters here is the otherness of these forces, and that they are all equally imaginary figures in a cataclysmic confrontation.[20]

The third chapter is also spun from a single incident. The narrator walks in Paris next to a trench being excavated by Arab workers. His desire to identify with them evokes three Europeans who attempted similar passages from their culture into another: Lawrence, Père de Foucauld, and Anselm Turmeda. The first two are better known, and I have spoken about them in the introduction. Anselm Turmeda was born in Majorca in 1352 and died in Tunis between 1425 and 1430. Just as Lawrence and Foucauld, Turmeda was a well-educated intellectual who chose the Arab over the European world. When he was twenty, he joined the Franciscans and traveled to Bologna and Paris to study theology. In 1387 he converted to Islam, took the Arab name of Abdallah (servant of God), married, and lived in Tunis the rest of his life. His most important work is *The Dispute of the Donkey and Brother Anselm* (1418), in which the donkey, a flea, and a louse (whose speech is reproduced in *Juan the Landless*) scoff at the pretended superiority of humans and demonstrate that they, and not humans, are wiser and have sharper senses.[21] In 1420 Turmeda wrote, in Arabic, an autobiographical text in which he tells of his conversion. These three men, Lawrence, Foucauld, and Turmeda, constitute a chosen ancestry for the narrator. They demonstrate that he is not alone in idealizing the Arab world above the European. He will follow in their footsteps, leaving Paris for northern Africa.

As the previous chapter signaled a geographical displacement, the fourth chapter moves back in time to show the control the Catholic church has had over thought in Spain for many centuries. The titles of the eleven sections of this chapter are in Latin, the language of Rome, a military empire, a language that survives especially in legal discourse and until recently as the sacred language of theology and Catholic ceremonies.[22] A page from a medieval chronicle tells how the church denounces soldiers who engage in homosexual acts at the public baths. The Inquisition's burning of homosexuals becomes a tourist draw and is described with the hoopla reserved for bullfights. A theologian—Vosk again—explains the benefits for the nation and the soul of the victim of the inquisitorial procedures. Franco, presiding over a purified nation, is celebrated as a saint. Alvarito reaches the blessed state of not needing to excrete. This parade of militant orthodoxies and fanatic enforcers leads the narrator to his aforementioned diagnosis: Spain suffers from constipation. It is a retort in the same language used by authorities, within the terminology of medicine, comparing the nation with a body as in the traditional image of the body politic. In this sense, the image is dangerous, since it grants the major premise, that there is such a thing as a shared body— and it is only one—which can indeed get sick. Readers should remember here that Goytisolo is not engaging in a debate but simulating it. We are invited not to be convinced by the arguments—they are far too exaggerated for that—but to take a step back and become completely aware of the implications of this debate. For years one of the factions has dominated and therefore has been able to pass off its version of reality as truth and its opponent's as heterodoxy and perversion.

In a similar way, capitalist society, competitive and hierarchical, presents itself as the only working model. The narrator advances in chapter five, in thirteen sections identified by roman numerals, a proposal for an egalitarian society. He ends with a reference to a ceremony that took place during the French Revolution, when the religion of mysticism was replaced at Notre Dame in Paris by a religion of reason. This was a mistake, affirms the narrator, and in his new society the only cult will be clandestine and dedicated to King Kong's phallus. Again, while there is here an appeal to the centrifugal, uncontrollable, and democratic nature of pleasure, the substitution of a new cult is a prolongation of previous modes of thought, and for it to be clandestine, it must conserve a supervising authority. Yet this is not a serious proposal for a new society—it reads at times as a parody of Castro's Cuba—but more a simulation of alternatives. *Juan the Landless* is not a presentation of ideas, but a representation of how ideas matter.

The narrator then turns to his own task, writing. To liberate himself sexually he must also get rid of the shackles of realism in his writing. As in previous cases, the point is not that realism in itself is despicable. Goytisolo has often expressed his admiration for one of the masterpieces of European realism, Leopoldo Alas's (1852–1901) *La Regenta* (1885, translated as *La Regenta*). What the narrator denounces is many critics' and most of the public's belief that a nineteenth-century literary strategy is the only natural and universal way of expressing reality and creating literature. He starts off with a spoof of the French writer Pierre Loti (1850–1923), who wrote exotic novels about the Middle and Far East. Loti was a prolific writer, who in many ways resembles Goytisolo. He expressed a longing to escape a rapidly modernized Europe, rejected all forms of constraint, celebrated the primitive, and highly valued eroticism. He is pilloried in *Juan the Landless* for his selling out, for becoming popular and accepting in 1891 a chair among the "Immortals," as the members of the French Academy call themselves. He did not, as Lawrence, Foucauld, and Turmeda did, have a life that corresponded to his writings. His exoticism was ornamental, his realism only superficial.

A different line of attack begins when the narrator escapes from the French Academy into the barren countryside, where he happens to hear the laments of someone who sings a poem accompanied by a guitar. This poem evokes a song that two friends of Don Quixote, the barber and the priest, hear in the mountains of Sierra Morena—even imitating the metric disposition of the strophes—in chapter twenty-seven of book one of *Don Quixote*. Cervantes's singer turns out to be Cardenio, a man who has been living in hiding, reverting to a natural state, and who is touched by a curious form of madness brought about in part by his extreme timidity. Cervantes's novel has been celebrated as the height of realism, but this episode is completely unrealistic in its implausibility. Here the savage madman intones a refined song that just happens to be overheard by Don Quixote's friends. A series of further coincidences will bring the three other parties involved in Cardenio's story together, and all their complicated stories will be solved later to everyone's relative satisfaction at the inn.

In *Juan the Landless* the singer is Vosk, the carrier of authority's ideology, and he laments that realism is under siege but consoles himself with the thought that readers still defend it. Further references to Cervantes's *Don Quixote* continue to underline the lack of verisimilitude of both books: Vosk appears to be a woman, just as Dorotea, another pivotal chance encounter, in chapter twenty-eight of *Don Quixote*, appears to be a man. Both are attempting to prevent sexual abuse from men, though the men in both books have different sexual preferences. The episode in *Juan the Landless* continues with references to *Don Quixote*, chapters thirteen and fourteen, in which Don Quixote comes across the funeral of Crisóstomo, a young man who committed suicide when his beloved Marcela spurned him. Crisóstomo and Marcela, together with other young men and women, had left their well-to-do homes to live the life of shepherds and sing their love songs in the hospitable hills and valleys close to their town. This is hardly realistic. Most likely, Cervantes was presenting a cautionary tale against believing that books which pretend to imitate histories of events that had actually taken place have a real referent. Goytisolo provides an example of such a text ("Where the port of Toledo is described, with other details which are necessary to understand this veridical story"), one which tries not to imitate reality but to imitate other texts that are considered truthful. This "veridical story" sounds plausible, except that it refers to the city of Toledo, at the center of the Iberian peninsula, as a seaport.

After an interlude in which Vosk ticks off all the defects of Goytisolo's writing, according to the theory of realism, the narrator takes a different tack to demonstrate Vosk's superficial understanding of literature. If first he had highlighted the unrealistic elements lurking in the masterpiece of realism, now he will bring out the dormant poetic element in everyday language. The narrator is led into a clinic, where he is to be brought into the fold of realist normality. The doctor who interviews him uses figurative language that the narrator interprets literally. When the doctor exclaims that he is so frustrated that his head is about to explode, it does. Thus, the fancy inventiveness of texts that simulate a veridical account of real events and the imaginativeness of standard language undermine the pretenses of realism à la Vosk.

The last chapter, divided into ten sections separated from each other by three asterisks placed in the form of a triangle, recapitulates the topics of the whole trilogy but moves further on in the last section, first resorting to a whimsical orthography (one of the orthodoxies he has thus far respected) and then switching into Arabic, first transliterated into Roman letters and finally in the Arabic alphabet. The reader, unless he or she knows Arabic, is left behind, the narrator at last having ended his communication and gone off to begin a new life.[23]

Notes

1. In a recent interview with Marie-Lise Gazarian Gautier, Goytisolo describes his relationship with two Cuban writers and Fuentes: "There are affinities between some Latin American writers and myself, which are stronger than with my compatriots, even though I was born in Spain. For instance, I feel closer to Cabrera Infante, Severo Sarduy, or Carlos Fuentes than to the majority of my colleagues in Spain" (139). In an interview with Emir Rodríguez Monegal, Goytisolo suggests that the Argentine Julio Cortázar's *Rayuela* (1963, *Hopscotch*) is a model for the type of open novel that he considers *Marks of Identity* (53). Carlos Fuentes includes a chapter on Goytisolo in his influential *La nueva novela latinoamericana*, only in appearance an odd decision. Fuentes explains that both Goytisolo and the best Latin American writers are struggling to create a new language, the Latin Americans against an inherited metropolitan, academic, and European set of expectations and norms, and Goytisolo against a barrage of established classics which celebrate essential values, such as purity, which are exclusionary and grounded in a series of questionable myths about Spain.

2. Most of the novel uses Alvaro as the focus of experiences and memories, offering his interpretation of events instead of many others which would be possible. Goytisolo believed at the time that adopting the point of view of a character who was similar to himself could offer a more genuine text. In an interview with Emir Rodríguez Monegal he calls his previous attempts to see the world through the eyes of people of different social classes and education than his an imposture (50). Reacting to the criticism that in the first edition of *Marks of Identity* most of the eighth chapter, dedicated to Alvaro's trip to Cuba, reveals a superficial and topical knowledge of that country, Goytisolo deleted most of this section in subsequent editions. Linda Gould Levine observes that this deletion made less understandable Alvaro's psychological development (*La destrucción creadora* 43).

3. The quotes are taken with almost no modifications from articles written to attack Goytisolo in Spanish newspapers such as *El Espectador*, *La Vanguardia*,

and *Pueblo*. Applying documents about the author to his protagonist raises the question of the identification of Alvaro as an alter ego of Juan Goytisolo. In an extended and thoughtful interview with the critic Emir Rodríguez Monegal, Goytisolo pointedly observes that there are autobiographical elements in Alvaro, but only because writers should write about what they know. He is, he claims, very different from Alvaro. If there is any relation, it is similar to that of a father with his son ("Destrucción de la España sagrada" 54).

4. Paul Julian Smith observes that *Marks of Identity* "re-enacts the Oedipal drama. It stages a return to the protagonist's origin and to the scene of his father's death, and it sets his quest for identity in the context of that origin and that death" (*Laws of Desire* 61). One could add that the novel goes on precisely to show that this Oedipal origin is spurious: Alvaro is the son of many deaths—not just his father's but also the peasants' near Yecla. Eventually, he escapes this familial determinism by inventing himself anew, cutting the umbilical cord created by this family romance.

5. The importance of Américo Castro's books in Goytisolo's view of Spain is profound. In an interview with José Hernández, Goytisolo declares: "Reading Américo Castro was for me absolutely fundamental, because I understood for the first time what Spanish history had been, and I could interpret correctly a series of facts which were meaningless otherwise" (343). Castro was born in Brazil to Spanish parents and grew up in Granada. He studied in Paris (1905–1908) and then returned to Spain to work in Madrid with some of the most outstanding intellectuals of the period, such as Giner de los Ríos and Ramón Menéndez Pidal. He taught the history of the Spanish language at the university in Madrid. In 1924 he was visiting professor at Columbia University in New York, and he later taught in Berlin. In 1936 he moved to the United States, teaching first at the University of Wisconsin (1937–1939), then at Texas (1939–1940), and finally receiving a position at Princeton, which he would hold the rest of his life. In this case, the biography reveals that Castro used his international experience—comparable to Goytisolo's self-banishment—to break away from the clichés about Spanish history. He posited, instead of a unique essence kept identical through the ages, a historical development that explains how the experience of being a Spaniard evolves from the conflictive but creative encounter of Christians, Jews, and Moors. For the relation between these two authors, see Michael Ugarte's excellent study "Juan Goytisolo: Unruly Disciple of Américo Castro" and Marina Martín's "Juan Goytisolo en deuda con Américo Castro: *Reivindicación del conde don Julián*." According to Christian Meerts, Professor Ayuso is a transposition into fiction of the important Catalan historian Jaime Vicens Vives (*Technique et Vision* 79).

6. This belated and literary victory must not be overestimated. In an interview with Julio Ortega, Goytisolo explains that Alvaro represents a frustrated generation: "*Marks of Identity* is, among other things, the expression of the process of alienation in a contemporary intellectual with respect to his own country. It is the exposition of a moral wound in a man of my generation who has had to live through one of the most sepulchral periods of peace in the lengthy history of Spain, a person who has been in the anomalous situation of growing old without having ever known youth or responsibility (as you well know, the Spanish people live in a perpetual state of legal adolescence since April 1, 1939 [the end of the Civil War])" ("An Interview" 4).

7. This episode has been exemplarily analyzed in *Laws of Desire* by Paul Julian Smith, who also points out the misogynistic behavior of the narrator as well as the rankling effect of the homophobic images in the novel (60–68). Part of the problem is that these attitudes and images that can offend some of us are not safely isolated in regions of the text where there is an obvious satire of Spanish myths and clichés, but proliferate in the region where the narrator's voice seems to seek the complicity of an enlightened reader. Goytisolo, though, is an equal opportunity offender, and one should not read into the text too close an identification between Alvaro and the author.

8. This would correspond to a mission Goytisolo had assigned for the Spanish novel two years earlier than the publication of *Marks of Identity*: "The rigidity of Spanish censorship has forced novelists to respond to the public's hunger for information by transposing into their works the outline of a reality opposed to the unreality of the newspapers; that is, to perform the witness-bearing that would normally fall to the press. . . . In this way, contemporary Spanish literature is a mirror of the obscure, humble, and daily struggle of the Spanish people for its lost freedom" ("Literature Pursued by Politics" 35–36).

9. For the many versions of this legend, see an informative article by Menéndez Pidal, "La leyenda de cómo se perdió España." This author, of conservative and nationalistic views, is variously ridiculed in *Count Julian*, but his erudition is mostly reliable, and he expanded greatly the knowledge of the Christian Middle Ages in Spain. Thanks to the paradoxes of intertextuality, he continues to speak from the pages of *Count Julian*, and a character who is supposed to represent him wanders through the heights of the Gredos mountain range, in central Spain, reciting chauvinistic poems and reminiscing about the victory of the nationalists in the civil war, together with another historian, Claudio Sánchez Albornoz, who extensively attacked Américo Castro's theories about the importance of Jews and Moors to the history of Spain (*Reivindicación*, Levine's

notes, pp. 191 and 257). For this controversy, see José Luis Gómez-Martínez's *Américo Castro y el origen de los españoles: Historia de una polémica*. Thanks to Goytisolo, Menéndez Pidal also gains a space in the bibliography of this book, in the inevitable proliferation of authority and erudition that *Count Julian* denounces.

10. For a sampling of the viciously negative image of the Arabs propagated by authorities in Spain during the 16th and 17th centuries, see José María Percival's "Asco y asquerosidad del morisco según los apologistas cristianos del Siglo de Oro."

11. If anything, this privileging of the phallus could be called "queer," in the sense in which this word is used in the new field of literary criticism which studies queer literature. Paul Julian Smith raises strong objections to Goytisolo's misogynist stereotypes, objections which I share, and his apparent reproduction in the novel of "the structures of patriarchy and its stereotypes of homosexual desire" (*Laws of Desire* 71), but he continues to show convincingly how Goytisolo's characters' unstable and theatrical roles avoid the trap of a reverse hierarchy (72–78). Brad Epps, in his superb essay "The Politics of Ventriloquism: Cava, Resolution and Sexual Discourse in *Conde Julián*," chastises the author's silencing of women and his reiteration of a traditional image of women as only desiring male domination and inviting male violence. Clearly, Epps is right. Goytisolo is not correct, nor, it is probable, would he want to be.

12. The editor and annotator of *Count Julian* in the Cátedra edition, Linda Gould Levine, labels the psyche of the narrator as "schizophrenic" (280). Ugarte refers to the "state of madness" of the narrator and "the deranged nature of his writing" ("Juan Goytisolo's Mirrors" 622). Stephanie Sieburth diagnoses that the narrator "suffers from a severe illness, a paranoid schizophrenia" ("Reading and Alienation" 83). Goytisolo himself contributed to this characterization when at a round table he referred to the text of *Count Julian* as an alienated, oneiric, and schizophrenic aggression (*Juan Goytisolo* [1975] 140). Abigail Lee Six makes of the term "collective schizophrenia," taken from the pages of *Juan the Landless*, the guiding thread of her book *Juan Goytisolo: The Case for Chaos*. José Ortega takes a similar view in his *Alienación y agresión*. In spite of the respect I have for all these authorities on Goytisolo's work, I strongly disagree with this characterization. To apply psychiatric terminology to a text is always a risk, but in this instance it would domesticate Goytisolo's novel by reducing it to a clinical symptom. This distancing within the self is rather related to what Lacan sees as one of the strategies of speaking about the self in order to understand what it is: "For in his labor which he undertakes to reconstruct *for an-*

other, he rediscovers the fundamental alienation that made him construct it *like another*, and which has always destined it to be taken from him *by another* " (*Écrits* 42, italics in the original).

13. Michael Wood accurately noted in his review of *Count Julian* for *The New York Review of Books*: "He [the narrator] is trapped in a vision of Spain which is no less conventional and sentimental than that of the academicians and bureaucrats he is pillorying, indeed which is the *same* vision—it is just that he is against it while they are piously for it. And *that* (Goytisolo implies) is what an occupied language feels like: not even the shape of your anger is your own" (40). Lynne Rogers, using Kristeva's concept of abjection, provides an insightful reading of this dependency as more a private issue—in the sense of a sorting out of the relationship of the son with his parents—than a political situation. Wood's and Rogers's readings can be seen as complementing more than excluding each other.

14. This episode can be compared with the famous scrutiny of Don Quixote's library by the priest and the barber in Cervantes's *Don Quixote*. Goytisolo has declared he was not consciously aware of this similarity when he wrote *Count Julian*, but he was "cervanteando sin saberlo" (writing like Cervantes unknowingly). The importance of this intertextual relation is that Cervantes used complex criteria for condemning some books to be burned and others to be saved—not just their realism—and Goytisolo shows an equally complex relation to his literary tradition. For an excellent analysis of how Goytisolo groups his authors and of the importance of authors who are *not* mentioned, see Sobejano's "Don Julián, iconoclasta de la literatura patria," also considering Andrés Sánchez Robayna's observations in "Góngora y la novela."

15. Gayle S. Rubin, in "Thinking Sex: Notes for a Radical Theory of the Politics of Sexuality," represents the levels of tolerance in American society by means of a circle, at the center of which are the categories of heterosexual, married, vanilla, bodies only, no pornography, at home, same generation, in a relationship, coupled, free, and procreative. At the outer fringes are homosexual, outside of marriage, promiscuous, nonprocreative, for money, alone or in groups, casual, cross-generational, outside of home, stimulated by pornography, with manufactured objects, and S/M (13). All the events in Goytisolo's fourth chapter occur at the outer fringe of this circle.

16. How disturbing these images can be even for friendly readers can be gleaned from an anecdote Goytisolo tells José Hernández during an interview in 1975. He recounts there that he sent copies of *Count Julian* to about thirty friends, as soon as the novel was published. After a year, only one person had responded

at all. This reader sent a letter in which he showed, according to Goytisolo, he had understood the novel. It was Américo Castro ("Juan Goytisolo—1975" 343).

17. Robert Spires in "Process as Product: *Juan sin Tierra*," provides a lucid analysis of the metafictional mode employed in this novel by Goytisolo.

18. For an excellent consideration of this topic as it has recently been played out in the United States, see Lee Edelman's "Tearooms and Sympathy, or, The Epistemology of the Water Closet." He quotes Norman Mailer, from an essay titled "Truth and Being: Nothing and Time," published in 1962, in lines which express perfectly all that *Juan the Landless* rejects: "if excrement is the en-forced marriage of Tragic Beauty and Filth, why then did God desert it, and leave our hole to the Devil, unless it is because God has hegemony over us only as we create each other. God owns the creation, but the Devil has the power over all we waste—how natural for him to lay siege where the body ends and weak tragic air begins" (568). Kessel Schwartz gives a reductive, yet useful, Freudian reading in "Juan Goytisolo, *Juan sin Tierra*, and the Anal Aesthetic," and also in "*Juan sin Tierra*, esperpento anal," included in the Espiral collection of es-says on *Juan sin Tierra* (81–93).

19. Paul Julian Smith comments insightfully on Goytisolo's inclusion of "queens" or daring transvestites in this series of threatening elements: "Goytisolo's praise of the queen can be linked to his critique of sexual identity and of psychological integrity. Like Goytisolo's fictional characters, queens have no fixed names or stable psyches; and both revel in parody and citation" (*Laws of Desire* 82). For the double function of King Kong, as a larger-than-life sexual icon and as a reference to Octavio Paz's *El mono gramático* (*The Ape-Gram-marian*), an essay of great importance as an intertext for *Juan the Landless*, see Ugarte, *Trilogy* 127–45.

20. Horst Rogmann was among the first to denounce Goytisolo's idealized and stereotypical image of the Arab in the novels of the trilogy. Both Claudia Schaefer-Rodríguez and Carmen Sotomayor pointedly denounce the author's unrealistic portrayal of the Arabs (Schaefer 53–70; Sotomayor 90–114). Smith writes concisely: "One would hardly suspect from the novels that many of the countries he describes remain subject to dictatorships as bloody and repressive as the regimes of Franco and Castro so mercilessly parodied in the trilogy; or that in at least one of them homosexuality is punishable by death" (88). Their criticism is well grounded, but it should be remembered that Goytisolo is not writing a realistic historical novel. His portraits of Spaniards, intellectuals, gays, children, and King Kong are equally distorted in the trilogy. If there is mimesis here, it is not of an exterior referent, but of the phantoms of the Western mind.

The recent flurry of anti-Arabic publicity in the United States since the war against Sadam Hussein and the bombing of the World Trade Center (which replaced Kong's favored Empire State Building as New York's highest phallic symbol) proves that images of the Arabs as uncivilized and primitive enemies of the West still roam Manhattan.

21. The original Catalan is almost completely lost, but a French translation has been published by R. Foulché–Delbosc in *Revue Hispanique* 24 (1911): 358–479.

22. They are: "Paulo maiora canamus" ("let us sing a loftier strain," Virgil, *Eclogues* IV.1); "Animus meminisse horret" ("The mind fears to remember," Virgil's *Aeneid*, II, 11; said by Aeneas at Dido's court when he begins to tell the story of the fall of Troy); "De vita et moribus"("Of the life and customs"); "Finis coronat opus" ("The end justifies the means," with echoes of Opus Dei?); "Salus populi suprema lex est" ("The well being of the people is the supreme law," from the Roman Twelve Tables, quoted by Cicero, *De Legibus* III, 3); "Monstrum horrendum, informe, ingens" ("A horrible, protean, and enormous monster," from Virgil's *Aeneid*, III, 658, referring to Polyphemus); "Hoc volo, sic jubeo, sit pro ratione voluntas" ("This is what I desire, what I enjoy, so let my will prevail over reason," from Juvenal's *Satires*, VI, 223); "Natura non facit saltus" ("Nature does not skip a step;" the complete quote is "Natura enim in suis operationibus non facit saltum" ("Nature in her procedures does not advance by leaps," Jacques Tissot, *Discours véritable de la vie, de la mort et des os du Géant Theutobocus* [1613]); "Video meliora, proboque, deteriora sequor" ("I see the best and approve it, but I follow the worst," from Ovid's *Metamorphosis*, VII, 19, said by Medea to herself when she realizes she has fallen in love with a foreigner); "Etiamsi omnes, ego non" ("All others, but not I"); "Ad augusta per angusta" ("To the greatest height through the narrow road").

23. While perhaps the most consequent reading of these last pages is one in which the Arabic remains impenetrable, here is the translation of the introductory lines and of the two concluding paragraphs, of which the first six lines correspond to the *Koran*'s well-known Surah 109:
You become like an Arab whose hands are first small and then big, who as a child and as a grownup goes to the Mosque and reads the surah you like:

> Say: You, the infidels!
> I do not adore what you adore,
> And you do not adore what I adore.
> I will never adore what you adore,
> Nor will you adore what I adore.
> You have your religion, I have mine.

You who do not understand,
Stop following me.
Our communication has ended.
I am definitely on the other side,
With the poor,
Who always find knives.

My colleague at Washington University, Mohamed-Salah Omri, who translated these lines for me—I have also used here part of Ugarte's version in *Trilogy* 147—tells me that the Arabic word for *pariah* or *poor* used by Goytisolo here rhymes with *knife*, making the last two lines striking.

At a colloquium in Buenos Aires in 1989, Goytisolo was asked if he wished to indicate he would abandon Spanish by ending *Juan the Landless* in Arabic. He responded that it was only a "procedimiento literario de ruptura brusca" (a literary technique of sudden ending), and a way of challenging his readers. Instead of writing "The End," he confronted them with unknown signs. He added at the Buenos Aires colloquium: "I am willing to abandon everything, except the language I have served as far back as I can remember" (Ruiz 67).

CHAPTER SEVEN

The Postmodern Goytisolo

A State of Constant Change and an Architecture of Inclusion

Since completing the trilogy, Goytisolo has published five novels: *Makbara* (1980, *makbara* is an Arabic word for cemetery), *Landscapes after the Battle* (1982), *The Virtues of the Solitary Bird* (1988), *Quarantine* (1991), and *La saga de los Marx* (1993, The Marx Family Saga), proving he had much to say even after Spain found her way into democracy. In an essay entitled "In Memoriam F. F. B. 1892–1975," dated 25 November 1975 and included three years later in his book *Libertad, libertad, libertad* (Freedom, Freedom, Freedom), Goytisolo wrote eloquently about the impact of Francisco Franco's death (20 November 1975). This immediate response to the demise of the dictator, which he first presented at the Library of Congress in Washington, substituting it for the lecture he had previously announced, reveals the significance of this event for him. Franco was the leader of the uprising that in 1936 started the civil war, the consequences of which would deeply mark the lives of several generations of Spaniards, and he became the head of a government which believed in controlling every aspect of its citizens' lives.

Goytisolo portrays him as a gigantic father figure, remote yet ever present, condemning all citizens to a permanent state of childhood, without a right to choose their government or decide what to read and write. Franco's effective control over the country, based on indoctrination, surveillance, and punishment, Goytisolo labels a moral genocide. He compares Franco to Dorian Gray, Oscar Wilde's character who remains young while his portrait ages, although in Franco's case, it is the general's image reproduced infinitely on postage stamps and official photographs that remains the same, while everyone else ages and dies. Against this resilience and self-perpetuation of the leader, which imparted a sense of stagnation to a country that was otherwise economically and socially on the move, Goytisolo reacted by exiling himself and writing the novels examined in the previous chapters.

"What I am today, I owe to him," he writes in this essay, in a sentence that is neither ironic in tone nor an expression of gratitude. Clearly, Goytisolo's writing had been profoundly concerned with and entangled in Spain's authoritarian regime. Where did he stand then, when Spain's dictator was dead and the country was finally able to plunge ahead into the political, social, and cultural transformation Goytisolo had desired for so long? What could he write about now? The sentence following Goytisolo's assertion that what he is he owes to Franco is disquieting. After all, his strong opposition to the regime determined many of the significant decisions of his adult life. He became a writer, he threw in his lot with the political Left, he was able to explore his dual sexual attraction, he read avidly, and he relocated to a Paris that was more hospitable and nurturing to him than Barcelona could possibly have been. Yet none of this first came to his mind to explain "what he is today." The full quote reads as follows:

Lo que hoy soy, a él lo debo. El me convirtió en un Judío Errante, en una especie de Juan sin Tierra, incapaz de aclimatarse y sentirse en casa en ninguna parte. (*Libertad* 17)
(What I am today, I owe to him. He made me a Wandering Jew, a sort of Juan the Landless, unable to belong or feel at home anywhere.)

As Goytisolo explains in this essay, Franco's death had come too late for him to return to Spain; he had become irreparably uprooted.[1] But he had not settled into an alternative identity based on an allegiance to a new state, party, or religion. After 1975 he frequently describes his roles as a person and a writer with the words *pariah* and *nomad*. As a social outcast he felt he had no obligations and no useful functions to perform in a global society to which he now turned with a vision as acerbic as his previous criticism of Spain. Because he saw himself as a wanderer, he did not wish to create for himself any permanent attachments. Against the tendency of institutions to unify and perpetuate themselves, he celebrated dispersion and discontinuity.[2] Against totalitarianism in any form, he reveled in fragmentation. Instead of the order of space, he asserted the fluidity of change and unplanned situations. For example, in *Makbara* he describes in great detail a primitive yet enormously complex marketplace which comes together in the morning and disbands in the evening, a place of transactions and fleeting social intercourse, an ephemeral architecture subject to whim, improvisation, and unexpected contrasts. To the uninformed eye, this market could seem mere chaos because there is no easily discernible and universal controlling principle, but a closer look finds local structures and behavior that are traditional and heavily scripted, such as the snake charmer's show, the medicine man's rituals, and the saleswoman's transactions. Each person in the market is allowed his own space to carry out his activities according to his own judgment. Similarly, in an essay about Istanbul, "La ciudad palimpsesto" ("The Palimpsest City," in *Aproximaciones a Gaudí en Capadocia,* a collection of essays published in 1990), what catches the eye of the narrator is not the usual monuments, but what he calls the urban forest, impossible to map fully, an ever-changing collage of people, architectures, activities, and times in history.

Goytisolo's preference for this fleeting, local, and playful architecture coincides with the position of one of the most celebrated texts of American postmodernism, Robert Venturi, Denise Scott Brown, and Steven Izenour's 1972 book *Learning from Las Vegas* (revised edition, 1977). For those authors the sprawling and irreverent buildings and signs of Las Vegas, where all hotels, casinos, and supermarkets compete for customers, create a more lively and approachable architecture than the austere, controlled, and functional buildings of modernism. They extol "the vitality that may be achieved by an architecture of inclusion" against "the deadness that results from too great a preoccupation with tastefulness and total design" (53). These words, in fact, perfectly describe Goytisolo's philosophy of inclusion and the intricate structures which characterize the novels of this later period.

If in previous novels there had been a concern with the signs of identity that had constituted his self, and a slow, even painful, realignment of a new chosen self with selected figures of the past, in these new novels the self is conceived as much more fluid, protean, and all-embracing. This new modality corresponds to what David Harvey defines as "the most startling fact about postmodernism: its total acceptance of ephemerality, fragmentation, discontinuity, and the chaotic" (44). Goytisolo sees in these characteristics—ephemerality, fragmentation, discontinuity, and the ehaotic—positive disruptions, liberating moves that counteract the unified and massive forces of global capitalism, the violence of superpowers, and the decay of centralized cities. One can apply to these newer novels what Harvey says of postmodernism: "It does not try to transcend [this fact of the acceptance of disruptive forces], counteract it, or even to define the 'eternal and immutable' elements that might lie within it. Postmodernism swims, even wallows, in the fragmentary and the chaotic currents of change as if that is all there is"(44). But, unfortunately, that is not all there is. In these new novels, Goytisolo looks at two particularly violent forms of devastation, war and AIDS, and asks what the individual can do when confronted by such powerful and superiorly armed opponents.[3]

Those readers coming to the newer works after having read the previous trilogy will recognize in them a continuation of the narrative style Goytisolo developed there, a style that has the freedom and lyricism more often associated with poetry than with the traditional novel. While *The Virtues of the Solitary Bird* and *Quarantine* revert to normal punctuation, the other three recent novels disdain capital letters and frequently leave to the reader the obligation of parsing the sentences. All five novels revel in abrupt transitions, intricate allusions, intriguing juxtapositions, and a meandering narrative line. Yet behind what some readers might consider chaos, there is the cosmos of a mature creator who, like Virgil in Dante's *Divine Comedy*, will lead readers to paradise and a new light if they are willing to dare the confusions of hell and the portrait of a profoundly disturbing contemporary world.

Makbara: Notes from Underground

The novel *Makbara* is composed of fifteen sections, which can be divided into two parts of unequal length. The first, and longest, running through the end of section fourteen, tells the story of a man whose ears have been eaten by rats and who walks through the city amidst the horror of those who see him.[4] He has grown up in northern Africa, but now lives isolated in Paris and in an American city, which is not identified but corresponds in many details to Pittsburgh. An angel has fallen in love with him, fascinated by his prodigious phallus.[5] This angel is of indeterminate sex, but is perceived as a transsexual who has gone from male to female. S/he is one of the two angels who were sent to Sodom and were assaulted by the men there, and s/he has never recovered from this disturbing encounter with human sexual desire. The funniest episode of the novel occurs when s/he visits a commercial exhibit for future brides, causing a flurry of irritated comments.[6] The final reunion of man and angel takes place in the sewers of the American city, but it is interrupted by a crew from a local radio station that is making a sensationalistic report on the underground city. Embarrassed and impatient, the heavenly authorities recall the angel, but s/he prefers to return to Earth and assume mortality.

Toward the end of the first part, readers discover that this story has been told by a storyteller in the market of Marrakesh.[7] This revelation may account for the differing versions of some events, the variant designations of the characters, and the story's several possible endings—all techniques that are part of the repertory of an oral narrator. What follows, and concludes the novel, is an extended description of the market itself. Clearly, the simpler and more human society of this market is counterpointed with capitalist markets of the postindustrial society, where the individual has lost contact with all stages of production and has become only a cog in an unencompassable wheel.[8] The African storyteller's narrative is an attempt to exert some control over a world that has become alien and forbidding. Here Goytisolo's favored image of the tourist bus reappears, but this time it is the Africans who visit the United States and fear the contamination of such a coldly efficient and puritan society.

The storyteller brings heaven and hell into his narrative: a bureaucratic heaven, which resembles a socialist country—dominated by the caprice of the First Lady and dedicated to the excruciatingly boring praise of the Leader—and the sewers, which are described with the dignified vocabulary used by archaeologists for Roman villages buried in lava. Between the heights of multinational organizations, Heaven being their pinnacle, and a labyrinthine substrata where pagan desire roams ignored, there is the surface of the Earth, a network of publicity and commerce where the individual exists only as producer and consumer. Both the man and the angel sell their bodies in order to live, he as a miner and s/he as a prostitute. *Makbara*, in its portrait of two fallen beings, tells the story of the destruction of the human race as such, and can be read therefore as a complementary version to the book of Genesis. The first line of the novel, "al principio fue el grito" ("in the beginning was the shout," with no initial capital letter), echoes the first line of the gospel according to John: "In the beginning the Word already was."

Another biblical echo, the proliferation of languages—Spanish, English, French, and Arabic—among the skyscrapers is a reminder of the divine punishment after the destruction of the Tower of Babel.[9] Goytisolo's substitution of a shout for the Word indicates a breakdown in meaning caused by an undifferentiated pain that contests a celebratory view of creation. As the storyteller wanders through the streets of Paris and Pittsburgh, his monstrous image imperils the confidence citizens otherwise have in the security afforded to them by the soothing power of familial names. Frequently repeated, these names of streets, stores, and products mark a perimeter where consumers can feel safe from the ravages of poverty, madness, and sickness. Against the planning and progress extolled by the media, the presence of the man without ears is a reminder of the limitations of human beings. Against a genesis that has led to an inhuman city, *Makbara* is a satire originating in a shout and ending in the emptiness of a blank page.

The movement toward the promised land of the marketplace in Marrakesh occurs because of the identification of the lovers with two celebrated figures of the European Middle Ages, Abelard and Heloise. Peter Abelard (c. 1079–1142) was a distinguished philosopher who was hired by the canon of Notre-Dame, Fulbert, to educate his niece, Heloise (c. 1098–1164). They soon fell in love and mixed the pleasures of learning with those of the flesh. Fulbert was incensed by Abelard's betrayal of his confidence and in 1119 ordered some men to assault him during the night and castrate him. Disgraced and a eunuch, Abelard became a Benedictine monk. He thus exemplifies explicitly the repression of the church against sex and passion. Yet his story does not end there. He continued to write, and his work became the target of Saint Bernard of Clairvaux (1090–1153), who managed to have it condemned by a church council in 1140. With his personal and scholarly life in shambles, Abelard could still enjoy one bright spot in his memory: Heloise, who had become the abbess of a monastery Abelard founded for her and who showed her intelligence, erudition, tact, and literary talent in a series of letters to Abelard which endure today as a testament to her merits and the power of love in the face of all difficulties.

As in his previous novels, Goytisolo has introduced here the anchor of a well-known referent to illustrate the depth and pervasiveness of the repressive forces he questions and defies. What is this cemetery of the title if not the eventual address of all human beings? In this cemetery and in this book, Abelard and Heloise now have as much freedom to talk as Fulbert and Bernard. While the latter are ignored by Goytisolo, Abelard and Heloise are rescued by the author as precursors in the never-ending struggle of human beings against suffocating institutions, of original thought against orthodoxy, and of love and writing against death. In section three of *Makbara*, when the lovers reunite in the cemetery, a few children are playing soccer on a clearing over old burial places. In several visits to Cairo, recalled in "La ciudad de los muertos" ("The City of the Dead"), an essay collected in *Aproximaciones a Gaudí en Capadocia*, Goytisolo discovers a teeming and, for him, fascinating city of living people who have taken refuge in the cemetery. In spite of the sterile impersonality of the contemporary age, life continues to flourish in the very house of the dead, with the same strategies and methods that occupied Abelard and Heloise.

Landscapes after the Battle: Juan in Wonderland

The playful and inventive novel *Landscapes after the Battle* is perhaps Goytisolo's most enjoyable and accessible. It is divided into seventy-seven brief sections, each with its own title. The sacred number seven, associated with creation and the pillars of wisdom can be read as an indication of the creation in second degree or the imitation of creation, and therefore a disturbing dispersion, which the novel describes. The starting point is familiar to Goytisolo readers. A writer, who lives as a recluse, imagines a radical transformation of Paris, completely taken over by immigrants and plunged into chaos by the sudden change of all writing from the Roman alphabet and French to the cursive flowing script of Naskhi and Arabic. This simple substitution for once puts the natives in the shoes of the immigrants, who must daily move within a labyrinth of names, instructions, and regulations that are incomprehensible to them. Once more, Goytisolo demonstrates the inescapable power of the written word and comes to the defense of those who are marginalized and undervalued because they belong to a different culture.

In this book, he displays a lighter touch and a higher degree of self-irony. The writer who imagines this humorous apocalypse has the same name, age, nationality, and address in Paris as the author of the novel. But he is hardly the brooding and earnest hero of Goytisolo's previous self-reflective novels. He has left behind the commitment to any ideology and participates, or imagines he participates, in a violent vindicatory movement for the Otekas, a people exterminated nine centuries ago by the Tartars and now neither mentioned in encyclopedias nor remembered in public conscience among the victims of history. The explanation for this change in allegiances is given late in the novel in a section titled "Del burgo a la medina," which can be loosely translated as "From the small and traditional [Spanish] town to the plural city," since Medina is the destination of the second most sacred pilgrimage of Islam and here stands for Paris and its multiracial, multicultural population. The writer's previous commitment to his cause, which he saw as central to the destiny of the world, and to the exploration of his wounded psyche, has receded before the evidence that from a broader view both his country's and his personal problems are minor and transient. His vision, he tells us, has become fragmented, his feelings, decentered.

Indeed, the character, as he himself notes in the last section of the novel, has multiple and seemingly contradictory aspects to his personality. He sees himself as a disenchanted revolutionary who is still capable of radical action; he fantasizes about erotic encounters with prepubescent girls that involve exhibitionism and masochism; he loses himself in the crowd of his working-class neighborhood, shunning the museums and intellectual watering holes for X-rated films at dingy movie houses; he reads and translates mystical poems by Sufi masters. Although his wife lives in an apartment across the hall from his, they communicate only by messages he slides under her door. A writer, he contributes pseudoscientific essays to the Madrid newspaper *El País* and pornographic letters to the Parisian *Libération*. There is no attempt made to reduce all these threads of personality into a single narrative which would explain them away as manifestations of a childhood trauma or a pathological condition. Instead of turning to Freud and the reductive Viennese family romance, we would find a more suitable model by looking at Las Vegas with Venturi's eyes and with his preference for the vitality of an architecture of inclusion. The writer in *Landscapes* celebrates the variegated nature of Paris, which he compares in a fitting gastronomic image to a many-layered pastry. Its flavor comes from the different ingredients, the successive waves of Jewish, Spanish, Portuguese, Turkish, Arabic, Afghan, and Bangladeshi immigrants. In the same way, the novel implies, a person can and must have many facets that may be unrelated to each other yet are all manifestations of his or her rich and heterogeneous nature.

As in many of Goytisolo's previous novels, a historical figure serves as the alter ego of the main character—if one can consider the shadowy and disparate traces of a character in *Landscapes* strong and powerful, to cite the etymological meanings of *main*. However, Goytisolo the writer finds an appropriate historical analogue for goytisolo the character, who writes his name without an initial capital, wanders in Paris in a film-noirish felt hat and raincoat, and is hardly more than a composite of recycled images, living a series of "weak truths" that do not claim to be universal, totalizing, or central. He blends in the text with Charles Ludwidge Dodgson (1832–1898), better known as Lewis Carroll, the pseudonym with which he signed *Alice's Adventures in Wonderland* (1865) and *Through the Looking Glass* (1872).

There is an obvious connection between Carroll's inventive, surprising, irreverent, and oneiric novels and *Landscapes*. They all waver between playful dreams and nightmares, rejoice at the absurdities of language, and reveal the brutal arbitrariness of authority. Alice has as much trouble keeping her shape as goytisolo his identity. While there is this deeper intertextual connection, the character goytisolo identifies with Dodgson for his fragmented life. Dodgson was the son of a clergyman and the oldest of eleven children, expected to follow in his father's footsteps. He attended Rugby School from 1846 to 1850 and graduated from Christ Church College in Oxford in 1854. For the rest of his life, he remained at the university town, lecturing and writing on mathematics.

He took deacon's orders in 1861, but was never ordained as a priest. He was well respected as a photographer, but Collingwood, his nephew and biographer, destroyed after Dodgson's death most of his numerous portraits of prepubescent naked girls. The Victorian mathematician, man of the cloth, and author of two of the best-known and most beloved children's books in any language had an immoderate attraction to girls who still showed the innocence of childhood but were budding into a more developed sexuality, the type of child Vladimir Nabokov (1899–1977) would later immortalize in *Lolita*.

Only in 1947 did any of these photos come to the public's attention, after Helmut Gernsheim discovered an album of some of these portraits of girls, posing seductively in scant and theatrical attire.[10] On the cover of the Spanish edition of *Landscapes*, one of the rescued photographs shows Alice Liddell, the daughter of the dean of Christ Church, in one of ten remaining portraits by Dodgson of the girl to whom he dedicated his most famous book. She stands against an ivy-covered wall, posing as a beggar in a torn dress, with bare feet, one hand cupped to receive the coins and another defiantly on her hip, her head tilted to one side, her look thoughtful, lively, and provocative. There is a resemblance in this portrait to Goytisolo's descriptions of fishermen and immigrant Arabs as sexual objects for a refined intellectual, the distance in social class making perhaps less intolerable the breach in the moral code.

Dodgson went to great extremes to secure his models. At times, he carried with him a suitcase of toys to attract his nymphets in the street, at a park, on trains, or in his preferred hunting ground, the children's theatre in London. He had transformed his bachelor's house into a playground, with dolls, mechanical toys, music boxes, and even a distorting mirror. Starting as early as 1867, he took photographs of nude girls, giving this dangerous practice up only in 1880, after a particularly frantic series of nude posings in July 1879. He kept lists of the girls he enticed, 107 by March 1863. The character goytisolo, dividing his time between mystical poems and exposing himself to young girls in the park or the library, is not far removed from Dodgson and can justly claim him as a kindred soul. The example, of course, is astutely chosen. Today, Dodgson would probably end disgraced or in jail. In his time, he sublimated his desire into a masterful series of photographs and two memorable books.

Dodgson's image cleansed by his biographer, the Alice of the photographs returns to reveal an unsettling dimension of repressed sexual desire both in his life and his writings. After the battle for liberalization of sexual mores fought in Spain toward the end of the Franco era, but general to the West in this century, we are better prepared to look unflinchingly at all the landscapes of the total geography of a human life—hence one of the many interpretations of Goytisolo's title *Landscapes after the Battle*.

Another aspect of the cover of the Spanish edition of *Landscapes* is instructive: both flaps contain a subway map of Paris. In a section titled "In the Paris of Forking Paths," an allusion to Jorge Luis Borges's famous story "The Garden of Forking Paths," the narrator recommends using the subway. The first paragraph is mostly a description of alternate routes to get to the place de l'Etoile, but, after the insertion of a line curiously containing two words beginning with capital letters, "O Aún ..." ("Or Even ..."), this is followed by a meditation on how the contemplation of the subway map can constitute a form of introspection. This passage can serve as a description of the novel itself, because it also consists of a network of texts that can be transversed in any direction (as the narrator suggests about the subway network); each section, as each subway station, has its own local existence, connected to the others more by contiguity than by subordination.[11] In a similar way, Lewis Carroll used a chess board as his metaphor for social relations in *Through the Looking Glass*. Each chess piece has a specific value, but one that changes according to where the piece is located in relation to all the other pieces, a value redefined with every move on the board. The difference, though, is that Alice can eventually leave behind her status as a lowly pawn and become a queen, while goytisolo moves in a network without a crowning square. All the elements the narrator finds in the underground—transfers, dead ends, one-way segments, among others—are aspects of the narrative of the novel, and the reactions prompted by the contemplation of the map—reminiscences, evasion, delirium—are also present, as well as the possible destinations—utopia, fiction, self-invention. Imagining this novel as an underground network also serves to remind the reader that the text is composed of pieces that are simultaneous and interconnected. *Landscapes after the Battle* is better contemplated in the totality of memory than in the obligatory succession of reading.

Imagining a social catastrophe by replacing the language of all signs; indulging in pseudoscientific, political, and sexual fantasies; trying on other personalities—all of these events in Goytisolo's Paris have the disturbing undertones that make Lewis Carroll's Wonderland a place where a smile and a frown can coexist.[12] On two occasions in *Landscapes* there is a curious change of register. In the first one, a section called "A Ella" ("To Her"), the narrator, who has kept at a distance from the character, suddenly wonders why the relationship he portrays of the character and his wife does not correspond to his, the narrator's, with his wife. This is a curious thought that reinforces and diffuses the autobiographical flirtations of the novel. As noted before, character and author share many traits, but here a difference is underlined, serving as a reminder of the fictive nature of the narrated world. To create the character goytisolo, it appears Goytisolo has used the distorting mirror Dodgson kept to amuse his nymphet friends.

In the second instance, in a section called "Variaciones sobre un tema de Nostradamus" ("Variations on a Theme by Nostradamus"), there is a reference to a momentous event in historical reality, the attempted coup d'état in Spain on 23 February 1981.[13] For a moment, the possibility existed that the battle for liberation would have to recommence, that an authoritarian regime would again rule Spain. Just as Alice on her chessboard could be affected by other pieces' moves, a political change taking place elsewhere could have deeply affected goytisolo in his bunker of the Parisian rue Poissonnière. The rebellion did not succeed—the recluse can continue his subway rides—but the postmodern celebration of fragmentation is tempered with the suspicion that locally, at least, individuals never cease to be dependent on vast forces beyond their control.

The Virtues of the Solitary Bird: Mystical Passages and AIDS

Two epigraphs open this beautiful, intricate, and moving novel. The first quotes two verses from "The Spiritual Canticle" by the Spanish mystic Saint John of the Cross (1542–1591), a poem he wrote in 1577 while incarcerated by fellow monks who opposed his attempts to return the Carmelite order to its original poverty and simplicity. The second epigraph quotes two verses from "Al Jamriya," a poem by the thirteenth-century Egyptian poet Ibn Al Farid.[14] Both mystical poets—one the greatest of the Spanish language, the other the most admired of Arabic—celebrate a spiritual rapture similar to alcoholic intoxication. Saint John writes, "In the interior wine cellar / of my Beloved I drank," and the verses of Ibn Al Farid complete his thought: "a wine which inebriated us / before the vineyard was created." Clearly, this is not normal wine, but an image for an experience that cannot be directly expressed. This is the first lesson of the epigraphs, since *Virtues* is a high-trapeze play of symbols in which every word points to experiences which language cannot completely grasp: death, love, violence, and transcendence. At the opposite extreme of a realistic novel, which pretends it can reproduce our experience of the world in a straightforward fashion, *Virtues* constantly reiterates that only through a devious path of mediating images can one aspire to understand human existence and its extinction.

The second lesson of the epigraphs can be drawn from the implicit connection between two people who lived centuries apart and in different regions of the world, and how they can merge into one voice. The ease in combining these two mystics can partly be attributed to a shared background between Al Farid and Saint John, an all-embracing tradition of mysticism that transcends any given religion. More specifically, there was a lingering presence of Islam in Spain at the time of Saint John of the Cross, convincingly demonstrated in Luce López Baralt's book *San Juan de la Cruz y el Islam*, which Goytisolo has often praised and acknowledges having used for this novel. But also, as *Virtues* asserts, there is a common mystical experience that can produce similar images. What matters is this continuity of sentences which indicates a continuity of life.

Completing the frame, the novel closes with a page titled "Acknowledgments," in which Goytisolo mentions the people and texts which helped him to prepare the novel, bringing us into his own wine cellar and showing us the texts that preceded and contributed to the one we read. Thus, the opening and the conclusion convoke other writers, as if the author wished to insist that he is only one voice in a polyphonic dialogue. In a letter he sent to the participants in a September 1989 congress in Almería dedicated to *Virtues*, Goytisolo wrote: "My intervention in

The Virtues of the Solitary Bird was . . . light: not that of a *deus ex machina* who intervenes, plans, decides, knows its secrets, but rather that of a scribe, almost a spectator" (*II Seminario* 1, my translation). The list of names reconvenes people already associated with Goytisolo's work, including, among others, his wife Monique Lange; the French critic Marcel Bataillon, the chronicler of Erasmian thought in Spain; José María Blanco White; Francisco Delicado, a priest who authored *La Lozana Andaluza* (1528), a richly textured description of the adventures of a prostitute in Rome;[15] the Baroque poet Luis de Góngora; José Angel Valente, a contemporary Spanish poet and a specialist in mysticism;[16] the critic Luce López Baralt; and Saint John of the Cross. The first incorporation of other names and texts, in the epigraph, is traditional, except for the smooth transition between the voices of Saint John of the Cross and Al Farid. The coincidence in expression between the two mystics, the continuity of their words, is not surprising from the point of view of the history of religion. The studies on the variety of religious experience by Evelyn Everhill and William James, early classics in this field, have convincingly demonstrated the identity of mystic experience within the framework of different sects and religions. For a literary critic and any traditional reader, the closing statement by the narrator is unsettling. These quotations acknowledged on the last page are said to be disseminated throughout the novel, but the narrator neither indicates the beginning and end of the quotations nor specifies their origin. No quotation marks, footnotes, or italics warn readers when they have passed from a verse of the chaste Saint John to exclamations of Delicado's Roman prostitute and then back to Goytisolo's own words.

These textual connections serve the same purpose as the arcades and bridges in some well-known short stories by the Argentine writer Julio Cortázar (1914–1984). In his stories, an unsuspecting character can suddenly find himself transported to ancient Rome, transformed into an axolotl, or walking away as another person. In one of Cortázar's most famous stories, "The Night Face Up," a young man has a motorcycle accident in a contemporary metropolis, Paris or Mexico City, and in his delirium finds himself back in what seems to be the fifteenth century, pursued by the Aztecs and becoming a sacrificial victim to the gods. The Aztec priests and the surgeons hovering around the operating table blend into one. Or perhaps this is a warrior of a rival tribe who falls into the hands of the Aztecs and, drugged in preparation to become a sacrificial victim, imagines he rides through an infinite city on the back of some giant metal insect and has a terrible accident. Cortázar's novels and short stories abound in these transitions that plunge characters and readers into worlds where the usual categories of time, space, and identity are malleable and suspect. In a similar way, *Virtues* both incorporates and erases difference. The many borrowed shreds may or may not be recognized by the readers as belonging to other writers and scholars, contemporary and centuries old, but no matter; together the fragments constitute one flowing, unified text. This is a rare case where an annotated edition would destroy a crucial effect of the novel. (One could imagine an English library like those appearing frequently in mystery novels, where, behind the rows of neatly bound books, entrances to secret pathways are hidden from the unsuspecting. Providing visitors with maps and placing large signs to show where all the secret doors are, together with instructions on how to operate their mechanisms, would be a misguided generosity.)

In his acknowledgments, Goytisolo affirms that the *Complete Works* of Saint John of the Cross are the backbone of the novel. Conceived as a body, the novel has a skeleton which the author borrows from another writer and which he fleshes out with material from still other writers. This openness to the other is selective, though, less whimsical than in Cortázar's stories—more a matter of willful choice than of accidental mingling. It affirms from its very structure the common destiny of human beings and their common language, but, in an extremely complex text, from the common materials and shared tradition *Virtues* will decant only a chosen few. Since this novel cannot be easily summarized, I will look briefly at the different narrative lines it pursues.

The narration begins with a voice that uses the feminine grammatical gender, the voice of a frequent visitor to a bathhouse in Paris where there are cubicles reserved for sexual activity. This establishment is loosely based on one which in fact existed in the rue Voltaire in Paris, frequented by a gay clientele.[17] This is, therefore, a transvestite speaking, and what he is concerned about is the arrival of Death. Personified as a woman, Death appears with a wide-brimmed hat, dressed in pink and yellow, with spiderlike legs attached to wooden stilts. The readers of

Makbara can remember her from the illustration on the cover of the Spanish edition of that novel, where she is seen as a giant figure dropping naked bodies from a great height over Paris. That cover, in turn, was a reproduction of a painting by the Belgian Félicien Rops (1833–1898), *La mort qui sème zizanie* (Death Sowing Discord). Rops qualifies well as someone whose work could be incorporated into Goytisolo's novel, for he was recognized as a master in printmaking but often trivialized because of the erotic and decadent content of his illustrations. This overflow of one book into another, of one form of art, painting, into another, writing, is part of the universal contamination which this novel exemplifies. The male body of the speaker has taken female attributes, his grammatical forms oscillate between feminine and an occasional masculine, and in a network of gossip and promiscuous sexual intercourse he enjoys communal pleasure, until this same openness makes him vulnerable to the scourge of AIDS.[18] He fears not only contracting AIDS, but also being isolated, controlled, and rejected, as a possible carrier of the sickness. As a Roman city with its life abruptly interrupted by a volcano's eruption, so the baths of the rue Voltaire are closed by the frequent visits of Death. Not even storytelling can wave away her hyperreal presence. What appears, therefore, to be superficial, a couple of Latinate expressions used by the person who runs the baths, and some pseudo-Roman decorations in their architecture, are uncanny intimations of a common destiny—the good life of a collectivity cut short.

The scene shifts to a resort where a group of specialists on mysticism has met to discuss "The Spiritual Canticle," but has instead encountered all sorts of obstacles and is sequestered in a place which resembles a stage, a balcony overlooking a painted sea with a fixed sun in the horizon, a place where history has ceased to flow.[19] This ominous location is an elaboration of the Writers' Union summer residence in Yalta in the former Soviet Union, which Goytisolo and Monique Lange visited in 1965, a visit described in *Realms of Strife* (233–40). Again we find the overflowing of one text into another, the uncontainable contamination. When he described this visit to Yalta, Goytisolo criticized the oppression of dissident writers by bureaucrats. He strongly denounced the insipid and regimented life of a state which treated many of its most creative citizens as though they were carriers of a dreaded virus. What is only a personal experience in *Realms of Strife* is expanded in *Virtues*, with echoes of Kafka and Genet, into a general condition that appears repeatedly in history. The assemblage hears a roar coming from a nearby stadium, so often and persistently that it seems to be a tape endlessly playing. This is a clear reference to the National Soccer Stadium in Santiago, Chile, which was used to house thousands of prisoners in 1973, after the violent coup that brought Gen. Augusto Pinochet to power. In this way, the isolation of suspected carriers of AIDS (the customers of the baths in the rue Voltaire) and of revisionist scholars (the participants in the congress on mysticism) is extended to dissidents both in a communist and in a fascist state, in the former Soviet Union and in Pinochet's Chile. In spite of their apparent diversity, they are sustained by the same backbone, in this case the skeletons of the same dead, the dissidents, the sick, the different, both in thought and in sexual practice. The same strategy of control used by communism and anticommunism is one more perverse manifestation of the struggle between free circulation and containment. What circulates freely here is an effective technique for violently controlling a society and suffocating any deviant behavior, of the body or the mind. What is contained is freedom itself.

In this oppressive resort, a male participant in the congress falls and is injured—he was probably pushed—is taken to a clinic, and becomes delirious. A doctor observes his every move and takes notes of the injured man's feverish words. Just as in Cortázar's story "The Night Face Up," the victim loses the anchor of his identity to the present and becomes identified with someone in the past, in Goytisolo's novel with Saint John of the Cross. The doctor becomes an inquisitor; the blood tests to determine the presence of HIV evoke the requirement of blood uncontaminated by Jewish or Moorish ancestors as a condition for social advancement during the Spanish Golden Age. This is the main connection established by the text between two characters, the protagonist (a thinly veiled Juan Goytisolo) and Saint John of the Cross. As usual, Goytisolo seems at least as interested in the life of his chosen alter ego as in this person's work. Saint John of the Cross's work is today revered in Spain, if perhaps little understood, partly because, as do all true mystical works, it speaks more to those who wish to open to the experience of the transcendent than to those who wish to understand a set of ideas. The attainment of such experience is difficult and runs against the grain of society, now as then. In spite of the fact that Saint John of the Cross was canonized in 1726 and declared doctor of the church in 1926, during his life he was considered suspect, and his teachings were seriously challenged. His texts have since become unattached from the struggle from which they sprang, in a characteristic social maneuver to hide the work involved in production.

When John was two years old, his father died. His mother managed to educate him and his two brothers by working as a weaver. Frequently reduced to begging and imploring help from richer relatives, a help that seldom came, she used the charitable institutions of the time—schools for orphans, hospitals—to educate and find jobs for her children. John entered a Carmelite monastery in 1563 and was ordained a priest in 1567, but he soon became unhappy with the increasing comfort of the order he had joined in the rich city of Medina del Campo. From 1565 to 1568 he studied at the university of Salamanca, where all classes were taught in Latin. When he returned to Medina del Campo, he found already there his friend Teresa de Jesús (1515–1582), the determinate reformer of the Carmelite order and a writer who has left some of the best-known and most profound pages of Spanish mysticism. Teresa recruited John for her reformation of the Carmelite order, to which he devoted the rest of his life.

These two admirable women, Catalina Alvarez (John's mother) and Teresa de Jesús, are unfortunately not part of Goytisolo's text. John's later life—after he had founded, inspired by Teresa, the male order of the Discalced Carmelites—is of more interest to him. John's previous brethren considered him a threat and resented the example of his austerity and mortification. In December of 1577 he was imprisoned in Avila by the unreformed Carmelites. While he was still in that city, he managed to escape, returning to his house to destroy documents and writings which could incriminate him. To destroy evidence of some of these papers, he ate them. Caught shortly thereafter, he was taken to Toledo, to a majestic monastery overlooking the river Tagus. There he was imprisoned in a windowless room, an old latrine, six feet wide and ten deep. Several times a week he was taken to the refectory and fed bread and water, on the floor. For almost five months, he was not allowed to change his clothes. After six months in that prison, a new guard took pity on him and provided him with pen and paper. In those conditions he wrote his most famous mystical poems, "The Spiritual Canticle" among them. How could Goytisolo not identify with him? Here is a writer who found his best lines while persecuted and incarcerated by church authorities, whose remaining work is only what has survived the catastrophe of censorship and self-censorship. His physical escape from prison, in late August, climbing down the wall of the monastery with a rope made from his shredded sheets, is less dramatic than his spiritual transcendence, his flight above pain, harassment, and resentment into verses of pure love that have endured long after all the Carmelite squabbles have been forgotten.

Here an important suggestion by Manuel Ruiz Lagos serves to illuminate the interplay between the different elements of this story. For Ruiz Lagos, this fall of the protagonist is an allegorical transposition of Goytisolo's painful revelation to Monique Lange of his bisexual orientation, with a marked preference for homoerotic sex ("Pájaros" 183). Goytisolo had revealed this to her in a letter mailed just before departing to the Soviet Union, where she joined him later, and the trip to Yalta was undertaken under the cloud of this new circumstance. This idea is useful in two ways. First, this fall can be connected with the myth of Icarus, the young man who wanted to reach the heights of heaven with the wings provided by his father and fell instead into the sea, when the wax that held the feathers together melted in the proximity of the sun. The ascent on extended wings, the melting at the climax of the hard wax into liquid, the fall—these images have been used before to represent the sexual act. But here the bird, instead of only standing in the place of something else, takes on a life of its own and proliferates in the text. "Birds" is a term for homosexuals in Cuba. A bird is a traditional conceit for the soul in its flight to God. The fallen protagonist participates in both the symbolic implications of a bird: he is a gay searcher of God. He is connected, therefore, with those birds of the rue Voltaire; with those who later in the novel are chased away from their meeting places in public parks in Havana and are interned in work camps, where the Marquise (a name the prisoners gave to Fidel Castro) disdainfully attends a ballet put on by the inmates;[20] and with those who die from AIDS. He is also one with Saint

John of the Cross, who is said to have composed a small treatise on *Propiedades del pájaro solitario* (Attributes of the Solitary Bird), a work unfortunately lost.[21]

The second way in which it can be productive to establish a relation between the fallen protagonist of the novel and the Goytisolo shaken after his revelation to Monique Lange is by being dissatisfied with simply making this identification and examining the process that produces it. We have seen how the fallen winged hero gives rise to a multidimensional bird, spiritual and gay. Now I would like to stress how the title of the book is misleading: this bird is not solitary. Instead, it defines itself precisely by its gregarious nature. Goytisolo's heterodoxes form a team, his birds a flock. Nobody in Spain has known so well how to invent for himself a tradition of dissidence as Goytisolo. At this stage of his career, he is in the company of an impressive group of men—they are all men— which includes Góngora and Blanco White, Cernuda and Delicado, Américo Castro and Jean Genet, Lawrence of Arabia and Saint John of the Cross. It is as if in his long search for personal truth, after going through the stage of social activism, after his passing fancy with Marxism and fashionable French linguistic theories, and after introducing an irreparable distance in his relation with Monique Lange when he could have feared finding himself in the solitude of hermits, he finds himself surrounded by other seekers of truth.

This is a story similar to the one told by Farid Ud-Din Attar, a Persian poet of the thirteen-century, in *The Conference of the Birds*, fragments of which are frequently incorporated in *Virtues*. Attar is another typical chosen ancestor for Goytisolo: he was a pharmacist and a mystical Sufi poet, persecuted as a heretic and exiled. In his extensive poem, remembered also by Jorge Luis Borges in "The Approach to al-Mu'tasim," a story dated in 1935 and collected in *Ficciones*, a large number of birds decide to go in search of the King of Birds, whom they know by the name Simurg, which means "thirty." They must traverse seven dangerous valleys associated with the following activities: search, love, mystical understanding, detachment and independence, unity, contemplation and awe, and total realization, with the complete annihilation of the self. Many birds abandon the search along the road, tempted by different passions or overcome by their weaknesses, their hopes undone. At last, those who have persevered reach the mountain where the Simurg lives, and they discover that only thirty birds have attained their goal. They realize they are now, and they have always been, the Simurg. I have not counted the number of ancestors and alter egos claimed by Goytisolo, but they may be approaching twenty-nine. In any case, the lonely bird of *Virtues* finds himself at the end of the novel surrounded by other exiles, harassed minorities, and outcasts, ready to take off, outfitted with new wings, on his way to the solitary mountain where the Simurg reigns.

There are other facets to *Virtues*. The protagonist remembers his childhood, memories of the Spanish civil war, with its factions, imprisonments, exclusions, and executions in the name of ideological cleansing. Finally, another thread in the story follows a character who visits a library to investigate books condemned in the past and now relegated to the "hell" of the institution, as if it were a perverse parody of the interior wine cellar of the epigraph.[22] What this scholar discovers is that, just as in George Orwell's nightmares, there are people whose only job is to destroy any subversive text and replace it with innocuous platitudes. This action mimics the mission of a hospital, especially its goal of identifying, controlling, and eventually destroying infectious diseases. A censored library, an inhuman hospital, a confining space, be it a cell for Saint John of the Cross or a stadium in Chile—all of these places subvert their original mission, becoming disseminators of violence, mendacity, and corruption. With inexorable rigor, the books in the library of *Virtues* are substituted with false versions, just as the hospital, the monastery, the summer resort, and the original Paradise—the homosexual baths in Paris—are contaminated and closed down, until all these institutions come to have no similarity any longer to the ideals on which they were founded. In this sense, then, Saint John of the Cross's most important work for this novel is his lost treatise on the attributes of the solitary bird, and Goytisolo's novel, four centuries later, comes to fill in the gap, offering to substitute his novel for the saint's treatise. If the many passages in *Virtues*—textual, chronological, spatial, and personal—prove anything, it is that the past continues to work in the present, still silencing, for example, one work of Spain's most revered mystic poet. It also proves that the present can restore, correct, and fight back the past, offering an inspired version of what Saint John of the Cross—Juan de la Cruz—could have written had he been Juan of Barcelona—Juan Goytisolo.

Of dispersion and chaos, of sickness and discord, of repression and forgeries, the many passages in the novel leave a testimonial to their own resilience. But Goytisolo also opens a passage through which the birds fly in search of their significance, which they must give to themselves to exist as a transcendent unity, which is One and Thirty at the same time. At this transcendental stage of the narrative there cannot be any footnotes obsessed with the private property of ideas and words because the text, unencumbered by name tags, forms the new body of the novel.[23] It is noteworthy, therefore, how adequate it is to gather at the end, in one list of twenty-one authors, the names of those who contributed to this novel. Not only does this procedure reflect the mysticism which pervades the novel—where the small self dissolves into a greater unity—but it also serves as a reminder that as a result of a long and admirable search for the uncompromising truth about his own self, Goytisolo has rescued and brought together a group of individuals who, with their life and work (and by concentrating on both, he goes against the grain of contemporary criticism), constitute a dissident community within which Goytisolo finally can fully recognize himself.

The Divine Novel: *Quarantine*

When Dante found himself lost in a dark forest and entered as a privileged visitor through the gates of hell, he found there a rigorously ordered universe, where at long last most of his enemies were punished and his friends rewarded. Even the sharp pain of seeing some of his former fellow citizens caught short in the accounting and condemned to eternal punishment for being envious, suicides, or gay did not detract from the deep satisfaction that absolute justice provided him. He never found innocent victims in hell. It was well organized and tightly run, and it had a splendid guide, the Roman poet Virgil, who was an old hand at visiting the underground. When almost seven centuries later Juan Goytisolo tours the same region, he finds many technical improvements—there are video machines and telephones installed—but where the neat spirit of scholasticism reigned in Dante's time, Goytisolo encounters now fuzzy logic and capitalism. The one consolation: the nether world is run according to the laws of Islam.

In forty brief chapters, a whirl of images and a multilayered, condensed language tell a lean story. A woman friend of the narrator has recently died of a heart attack. He and his wife are very much affected because they had seen her full of life briefly before her death. The narrator met her in New York, when he was teaching at New York University, and she began to translate some of his works. They often discussed literature, especially Dante. In sympathy, the narrator declares that he too is now dead and follows his friend for the forty days in which the soul, according to Islamic teachings, is in transition to a final destination. Because in Spanish the word for soul, *alma*, is feminine, and she is the transcendental tourist, the narrator and his friend are not only reunited spiritually but are fused into one gender, at least in grammar, generating a text in which attributing an action to a particular subject is not always possible. This slippage is only one of the consequences of categories that begin to fade away, as the restrictions of space and time no longer apply beyond the grave.

The narrator takes a guided tour of hell, where he gleefully finds appropriate punishments doled out to many of his antagonists. For example, the Spanish scholar Menéndez y Pelayo—admirable for his formidable erudition, but frequently berated by Goytisolo for his conservative views and often parroted by subsequent critics—is simultaneously in hell and heaven. Menéndez y Pelayo is allowed to sit among the chosen in glory, but only as a spectator, condemned for all eternity to see Blanco White among the most exalted of the saved. Similarly, a noted inquisitor, Tostado, must endure the glorification of the quietist Miguel de Molinos, and Tostado's Arab counterpart suffers the salvation of a Sufi mystic. Another inhabitant of hell is in fact still alive; he is described as a trivializer who transmutes ideas into money and produces an incessant flow of disastrous novels, plays, and essays. The clue to his identity is given by the inclusion of the Spanish saying "zapatero, a tus zapatos" (cobbler, to your shoes), which is also offered in the version "caballero, ¡a tus caballos!" (rider, to your horses!). Goytisolo is referring to Fernando Savater, who has frequently written about horse racing and who angered him with some anti-Arab declarations during the Persian Gulf War.[24] A more cryptic allusion is to some trifling figures in the offices of a dark house, dressed up as rugged sailors. As the Catalan critic Pere Gimferrer reveals in his review of this novel, this is a reference to the publishing house of Seix Barral, in Barcelona, Goytisolo's publishers for many of his novels and directed until 1970 by Carlos Barral, a well-known enthusiast of sailing.

The narrator materializes, now dead, in his Paris apartment, where his wife does not appear at all surprised by his new condition. He receives a notice that he must present himself to a tribunal which will evaluate his life after he responds to three questions on the following topics: Sufism, the exact date on which he began masturbating, and his bowel movements. This note is signed by doctors Nakir and Munkar, two of the examiners of the underworld.[25] *Nakir* means *horrible* in Arabic and is a word used to express reproof, but the narrator is not worried and feels he has studied the Sufis well enough, can remember the required date, and has a medical certificate to prove his bowel movements are regular and normal. Beyond that, of course, and more serious, looms the question of the value of his life and writings. It has been suggested that Goytisolo has had a remarkable ability to direct the criticism of his work along certain paths broken first by his own acute readings of his work (Martín Morán, "Instrucciones" 99). In this case, he is addressing the ultimate reader, God, slipping a few words into his divine ear before God makes up his mind. Nakir and Munkar are rather pleased with Goytisolo, whose life they have examined and whose work they know by heart. And this is their verdict:

En medio de la chatura de unos tiempos míseros y uniformes, tan faltos de enjundia como llenos de paja, su vida hecha texto tenía al menos el mérito de la pasión contaminadora, el poder revulsivo de la imaginación y el dislate. (24)

(In the midst of the mediocrity of a miserable and insipid time, as lacking in intelligence as full of hot air, his life made text at least had the merit of contaminating passion, the revulsive power of imagination and nonsense.)[26]

In this rehearsal for his real death and judgment, as intimated in chapter thirty-seven, the narrator, who seems to have written all those books signed by Juan Goytisolo, anticipates a favorable sentence by the effect he has had upon his readers.[27] This could appear a curious line of defense for someone who has defined himself repeatedly in his works as a loner and an exile of society. Ultimately, nevertheless, the good he has done to others is what counts, the fever he has transmitted to help fend off the moral sickness of our times. His compassion behind the gruff exterior is smoked out in the proximities of hell.

If this hell of his imagination has an Arabic flavor, even though presided over by Dante, it is because at least since the study of Miguel Asín Palacios in 1919, translated as *Islam and the Divine Comedy*, it has been known, though not sufficiently recognized, that Dante was greatly helped in the construction of his fictive universe by his knowledge, direct or indirect, of Arab writers, especially the work of Ibn al-Arabi from Murcia.[28] It should come as no surprise to readers of Goytisolo's works that in *Quarantine* he reaches again into the past to find a compatible person with whom he can identify. In this case his alter-ego is al-Arabi, a distinguished, prolific, and profound Sufi mystic, born in Murcia in 1165, at a time when more than four centuries of Arabic dominance in the Iberian peninsula had produced a thriving center for European and African culture in southern Spain. Ibn al-Arabi came from an affluent and religious family. He studied law and Islamic theology in Seville and Cordoba, had the crucial guidance of two elderly woman teachers, was examined and admired by Averroës, and soon had an international reputation as a mystic of unusual depth.[29] When he was thirty-three years old, after repeated brief trips to northern Africa, he started a pilgrimage to the East and finally settled, when he was sixty years old, in Damascus, where he died in 1240. Around 150 of his books still survive, among them *The Seals of Wisdom*, cited by Goytisolo in *Quarantine*. His treatises on mysticism are extensive and continue to be studied today. His poetry, especially the love poems, are notable and well known in the Arabic world. One of Ibn al-Arabi's most famous poems, is quoted in chapter thirty-four of *Quarantine*:

My heart is capable of every form,
A cloister for the monk, a fane for idols,
A pasture for gazelles, the pilgrim's Ka'ba,
The Tables of the Torah, the Koran.
Love is the faith I hold: wherever turn
His camels, still the one true faith is mine.[30]

The all-embracing love of the mystic for all forms which reflect the Creator is similar to the novelist's inclusive world. In chapter seventeen, Goytisolo refers to this unity as expressed by Ibn al-Arabi. One example, among many I have found in Ibn al-Arabi's work, is the following quote from *The Seals of Wisdom*:

The Cosmos is illusory, without any real existence, and this is what one means by the Imagination. That is to say, you imagine that the Cosmos is something separate and autonomous, outside the Real, when in truth it is not. Have you not observed that shadows are connected to the one who casts them, and would not its becoming separated be absurd, since nothing can be separated from its own essence? Therefore, know your own self, who you are, what is your identity and what your relationship with the Real. (71–72)

Undoubtedly Goytisolo has heeded, even before reading al-Arabi, this admonition to know himself and discover his identity. What he has found is that the relation with the Real involves retiring into what is usually understood as a private self—Juan Goytisolo writing in the kitchen of his apartment in Paris—in order to discover how all the world flows in again through his pen. The imagined distancing, the eremitic character of the writer, gives way to a much deeper and more real interconnection of shadows which forms the One—a book in the first instance, a larger Self beyond it.

From this experience of unity comes the narrator's compassion for the suffering of others, first for his suddenly deceased friend, and then for the many victims of a war which started after Goytisolo had already begun *Quarantine*: the Persian Gulf War, which was precipitated by the invasion of the small Arab state of Kuwait by the neighboring Iraq led by its president Saddam Hussein. A broad coalition led by the United States forced Iraqi forces to retreat after a devastating war that lasted forty-three days, from 16 January to 28 February. Five weeks of intensive air raids culminated in a ground war which began at 8:00 P.M. on 23 February and lasted exactly one hundred hours. Unlike the one hundred cantos of Dante's *Divine Comedy*, which led to the beatific vision of Paradise, these hours of battle led to burning oil refineries, craters from air raids, smoke from destroyed neighborhoods, and at least one hundred thousand people dead, presenting an image of hell to the hundreds of millions of spectators who had followed the conflagration across the world on their television screens. A city beloved to all readers of *The Arabian Nights*, Baghdad, lay in ruins. Goytisolo was horrified, and *Quarantine* is his anguished cry at all the loss and pain he saw during these days and has seen throughout his life. In chapter eight, a tidal wave of blood advances toward his house on the second day of the war, 17 January. In chapter twenty-five, he finds among the victims his own mother. She represents the victims of all wars, anywhere. If we could only identify with them as the mystics do, Goytisolo suggests, each one of them would be to us as a mother. And in a minor chord of requiem, there are in chapter fourteen fleeting mentions of the Argentinean novelist Manuel Puig and the Cuban novelist Reinaldo Arenas, both recently departed to their own forty days of purification. The novel speaks with the loving desolation of a Kaddish, with the ontological melancholy of the *ubi sunt*. It is in the nature of a monument to the fallen, including Goytisolo's future self.

Untimely Meditations: The Marx Family Saga

In one of his most memorable essays, "On the Uses and Disadvantages of History for Life," Friedrich Nietzsche distinguishes between several different ways of relating to history. Unlike all other animals, who live mostly immersed in an eternal present, human beings, using their imagination and language, eagerly remember the past and anticipate the future, becoming oblivious to what is in front of them at the moment. Some people lose themselves in the past where they roam as hunters or collectors and wish to plunder that past; others feel the need to conserve the past, and they become antiquarians; still others search in the past to find monuments with which they can identify. Only few, according to Nietzsche, use the study of history properly to understand better the present and prepare adequately for the future. Goytisolo has practiced a "monumental" approach in the past, but in this latest book his relation with history has changed: there is less a search for a kindred exemplary figure and more a need to understand critically the roots of the present to shape the future better.[31]

Goytisolo's *La saga de los Marx*, a novel about Marx and his family, goes out of its way to indicate that it does not belong to any of the first two categories.[32] The author does not wish to compose a historical novel to obtain the movie rights and become immensely popular—he does not wish to profit from the past—nor does he wish to reproduce the data in the most pristine and exact fashion possible. In fact, to avoid any suspicion of commercialism, this is a novel which pretends never to have been published at all. As the narrator presents his story, he has been commissioned to write Marx's fictionalized biography by an editor, Mr. Faulkner, who is desperately trying to bring the narrator, someone who is much like Goytisolo, into the mainstream. Enough of his experiments, implores Mr. Faulkner, enough of his cryptic novels, which only satisfy a clique of devoted readers, and enough of his Moorish ramblings. The editor urges the narrator to give his readers what they want: facts, descriptions, and normal punctuation, and to get rid of his male chauvinism, his blindness toward the oppression of women under the patriarchy. Mr. Faulkner recruits a feminist from California, Professor Lewin-Strauss, to enlighten the narrator in a fiery encounter characterized by his lame and interrupted replies to her pointed allegations.

The narrator, in the first installments of the manuscript he is sending to Mr. Faulkner, has begun to describe the Marx household and has repeatedly referred to their maid, Helena Demuth, known familiarly as Lenchen, with the word *faithful*.[33] He does not see that she is an exploited woman, and cannot understand that Marx had a blind spot when it came to his own family, in particular, but also, in general, to the situation of all women? The narrator is so caught up with his characters, so fascinated by their voices, that he has no time to stop to provide detailed descriptions. To please his editor, he copies a few descriptions from other sources and at last, in exasperation, resorts to attaching to his text a photograph of Lenchen to avoid describing her.[34] Finally, aware that he will satisfy neither Mr. Faulkner nor Professor Lewin-Strauss, he gives up and throws the whole manuscript into the wastebasket. But, of course, readers know better: the editor will love this book, and so will the professor.

Within this ingenious frame lies one of Goytisolo's most daring novels. The main premise is that Marx and his family are still alive, witnessing from their apartment in London how the regimes based on his ideology have collapsed while capitalism has triumphed, making a mockery of his predictions of the inevitable victory of the proletariat. The narrator stalks Karl Marx (1818–1883) as an investigative reporter would and is even invited to a party the Marxes throw to celebrate moving to a new home.[35] At the same time, his editor, Mr. Faulkner, has gone ahead with the production of a television dramatization of this same party, focusing on Marx's wife, Jenny von Westphalen (1814–1881), a well-to-do woman from Trier who found herself thrown into exile—in Belgium, France, and England—and into dire poverty by being married to a philosopher and political activist. And her story is, indeed, an important part of the novel. Goytisolo includes in *La saga de los Marx* a few pages of the script, allowing us to enjoy their corny melodrama.[36] These scripts, nevertheless, have enough of a kernel of truth in them to convey the sadness Jenny von Westphalen may have felt for the contrast between her expectations and her reality. Goytisolo includes a chilling letter in which she describes the poverty of her family in London, which ultimately contributed to the early death of four of their seven children. To increase her worries, Marx had a roving eye and fathered a child with Lenchen. The paradox here is that the television script intensifies the melodrama at the same time that it betrays it, by putting the enjoyment of the spectator before the compassion for Jenny's struggling life. The commercial packaging and distribution of her life becomes one more example of Marx's observations about how the workers do not reap the benefit for their labor and become alienated from the final product. In this case, Jenny von Westphalen's life becomes for Mr. Faulkner raw materials to be ransacked in an always underdeveloped and helpless continent: the past.

Goytisolo springs to the defense by cleverly pointing to the inanity of the television production and allowing Jenny to reach today's readers directly by the transcription of her letter. Also, the narrator interviews her, visits her house, and reconstructs her joys and sorrows. He seems, after all, to have heard some of Professor Lewin-Strauss's recommendations. Attempting to provide a balanced account of Jenny's life, the narrator remembers her contribution to her husband's work, not only serving as an efficient secretary—Marx's handwriting was almost illegible, so she had to transcribe his work—but also heroically keeping the home afloat. As a result, she appears more important and oppressed than perhaps Marx would have been willing to grant, but less enraged, bitter, or downtrodden than Professor Lewin-Strauss would have made her out to be. Especially effective and moving is the highly cinematic sequence in which the narrator envisions the lives of Marx's surviving three daughters, two of them unhappily married and suffocating in their homes, the third and youngest—a political activist and a translator of Flaubert—thwarted by Marx in her first love and ultimately a suicide. The crumbling of the empire built invoking his teachings was preceded by a domestic collapse of his family's illusions, both catastrophes occasioned by a blindness to the evils of authority. Once again, Goytisolo has asked the question of the use of ideas in the practice of life. Once again, he has not found it sufficient to read what his characters wrote but has examined how they lived. The verdict is not altogether negative. In spite of the patriarch's blindness and silence regarding the exploitation of women, the love, loyalty, and tenderness in this family redeem it. But what about the ideas to which the whole family devoted its existence?

By a deft alternation of brief quotes, interviews—some of them based on historical facts—and opinions expressed by the characters, the novel clearly supports the idea that the kernel of authoritarianism in Marx's thought and life developed into a monstrous dictatorial machine where human beings were sacrificed in the name of supposedly scientific prognostications of a future better world. The anarchists, who opposed hierarchical authority and were Marx's nemesis, and who played an important role in Spanish history, are presented favorably, especially Mikhail Bakunin (1814–1876). He, as Marx, is still alive in Goytisolo's novel and roaming Europe, performing numerous pranks to startle people into a recognition of their exploited condition. And this is the punch: Marx was right. While he was not much of a prophet, he diagnosed correctly, according to the novel, the misery capitalism inflicted and continues to inflict on the cities. The plight of the proliferation of the unemployed and the homeless, drug addicts, criminals, and destitutes in contemporary metropolises all over the world, contrasting with huge fortunes and enormous salaries for a few, shows that the conditions Marx wished to analyze have not greatly changed.

Goytisolo, who in the past has so often sided with outcasts and marginal figures, stands once again next to someone currently despised, betrayed, and neglected, the improbable figure of Karl Marx. As the novel draws to a close, the narrator participates in a televised forum, a format frequently incorporated by Goytisolo into his novels and which serves the purpose of showing how behind the facade of dialogue and authority hide passions, provincialism, and ignorance. Above the panelists looms a large photographic image of Marx, who seems to listen with pained astonishment to the participants' opinions. Only with the narrator does he communicate fraternally, showing to him, by raising his bushy eyebrows, his exasperation.

La saga de los Marx is arguably one of Goytisolo's best novels, brisk, humorous, inventive, compassionate, and ultimately profound. But it stands on the shoulders of a lifetime of innovative writing and uncompromising exploration. From the stilted *The Young Assassins* to the sure-handed technical prowess of this most recent book extends a life devoted to quality in literature and justice in life. A true creator redefines his territory and strikes his own paths. This is clearly what Goytisolo has done, fusing life and work, private and public, past and present, Europe and the Arab world, in his own admirable saga, only briefly described in this book.

Notes

1. This condition of an almost imperceptible erosion of the ties that bind exiles to their countries is clearly shared by many in this century and in the past, and is one of the most insidious afflictions imposed by dictatorships on those

who oppose them from abroad. The dictatorship of Augusto Pinochet in Chile, which lasted from 1973 to 1990 and was inspired by Franco's model, kept me away from my own country long enough to make me feel like a virtual tourist in my own homeland when I returned briefly after many years of absence and with a foreign passport. What matters in this discussion, though, is not the experience of exile, but what Goytisolo does with it, how he transforms his loss into our gain with his texts.

2. Goytisolo's conception of an opposition between a molecular or molar society, compact, hierarchical, and unified, as opposed to a more desirable condition of nomadism, with ephemeral and horizontal relations, and in a situation of fragmentation, is clearly reminiscent and owes some of its terminology to the ideas proposed by Gilles Deleuze and Félix Guattari in *Anti-Oedipus: Capitalism and Schizophrenia* (first published in French in 1972) and fully expounded in *A Thousand Plateaus: Capitalism and Schizophrenia* (first published in French in 1980). It should be kept in mind, though, that this is not a case of a mere intellectual borrowing of fashionable ideas, but more of an elective affinity, since Deleuze and Guattari's ideas coincide with concepts Goytisolo had been developing in his essays and novelistic world for many years before.

3. I have written in further detail about Goytisolo's relation to architecture and postmodernism in my articles "The Different Architectures of Metafiction in Juan and Luis Goytisolo," "Theory and Contemporary Autobiographical Writing: The Case of Juan Goytisolo," and "El autorretrato postmoderno de Juan Goytisolo."

4. José Luis Alonso-Hernández, in a detailed Freudian reading of *Makbara*, sees in the man's lack of ears a symbol of his inability to hear language, which contains all rules of the superego, and of his openness to the Id (62). The man, though, can still hear perfectly well, and his lack of ears appears to have only an aesthetic effect. Nevertheless, Alonso-Hernández is right in noting that this man is not attuned to obey the rules and regulations of conventional society, and his lack of ears may indeed be read as a symbol of his independent spirit.

5. Much of the vocabulary used to describe this prodigious phallus reveals the memory of Goytisolo's reading of the Cuban José Lezama Lima's *Paradiso* and of the Spaniard Joaquín Belda's erotic novels, which Goytisolo studies in "La metáfora erótica: Góngora, Joaquín Belda y Lezama Lima," an essay in *Disidencias* (1977). Carmen Sotomayor, quoting in her support Linda Gould Levine and Claudia Schaefer-Rodríguez, criticizes strongly Goytisolo's portrayal in *Makbara* of the ideal woman as an idolizer of the phallus (*Una lectura orientalista* 154). If the angel is understood as a woman, they are correct in this

reading. I believe, though, that as a transsexual s/he is not part of a heterosexual couple—and does not therefore represent woman—but of a gay relationship, and partakes of a form of masculine eroticism.

6. Luce López Baralt observes correctly the importance of Caribbean authors, especially Lezama Lima, Severo Sarduy, Cabrera Infante, and Luis Rafael Sánchez, for Goytisolo's irreverent humor in *Makbara* and *Landscapes After the Battle*. It is unlikely, though, that this humor is as unconcerned with a serious critical goal as she portrays it to be in "Juan Goytisolo aprende a reír."

7. For a Derridean reading which stresses the importance of the storyteller in the privileging of orality over writing, see Annie Perrin's "Pour une écriture-lecture-audition: *Makbara* ou la voix retrouvée."

8. Similarly, in chapter three of *Pueblo en marcha* (1962), Goytisolo's idyllic chronicle of revolutionary Cuba, he includes a detailed description of the market in Manzanillo, adding that wherever he goes, visiting the marketplace is for him a high point of his trip, *una fiesta*.

9. Ahmed Benremdane observes that Goytisolo is nevertheless careful to make words in Arabic comprehensible in a general sense to his readers, providing either an explanatory context, translations, or paraphrases or making clear that these words are only repetitions in Arabic of what has already been said in Spanish.

10. Gernsheim published some of Dodgson's photographs in *Lewis Carroll, Photographer*, in 1949. There is a beautiful edition of the photographs, together with charming and pre-Freudianly sensuous letters to his young models, edited by Guido Almansi, *Lewis Carroll: Photos and Letters to His Child Friends*. Most of the information about Dodgson's photographic passion given later in this chapter comes from an essay by Brassai contained in this volume.

11. José Manuel Martín Morán provides an excellent and careful structuralist description of *Landscapes* in *"Paisajes después de la batalla.* La verdad, la ficción y el vacío," showing convincingly that the novel has a tight organizing force behind its apparent randomness and chaos. That this is not easy to see can be observed by reading Robert Kiely's review of *Landscapes* in the *New York Times Book Review*. It is a positive review, but Kiely is clearly baffled by the novel, which he describes as "brilliantly peculiar" and "flamboyantly eccentric," concluding that "Mr. Goytisolo's choice is to write a fraudulent novel without a hero and without a plot."

12. For the many possible implications of Carroll's adventures of Alice, see Peter Heath's *The Philosopher's Alice*. Currently there is only one annotated edition of a Goytisolo novel, Linda Gould Levine's excellent edition of *Count*

Julian. Landscapes is a book that will probably reveal its depth after a process of thorough annotation, but then some of the breeziness of the prose may suffer. It is a book that demands a good-humored but extremely erudite reader.

13. For further details on the relation of this novel with Spanish society in the late 1970s and early 1980s, see my essay "Writing After the Battle: Juan Goytisolo's renewal."

14. On Al Farid as well as other poets of the mystical tradition in Islam, see the extensive and useful study by Annemarie Schimmel, *As Through a Veil: Mystical Poetry in Islam.*

15. As Goytisolo reminds us in his essay "Notas sobre *La Lozana Andaluza*," included in *Disidencias*, Delicado's book was published anonymously in Rome and was ignored in Spain for centuries, except for a few denigratory remarks by critics scandalized by the freedom with which Delicado portrays sexual mores. Goytisolo, appropriately, considers *La Lozana* an "obra maestra" (39), a masterpiece.

16. Valente is the editor of the *Spiritual Guide* (1675) of Miguel de Molinos (1628–1696), a Spanish priest who became popular in Rome preaching a form of quietism, that is, a natural silencing of the mind which would make the individual experience his or her oneness with God. Molinos owed many of his practices and ideas to Saint John of the Cross. Because he relegated to a secondary position traditional rituals, prayers, and the intercession of priests, he was attacked by Jesuits and Dominicans. They managed to defame his reputation and had him arrested in 1685. Tried and condemned, he died in the prisons of the Inquisition in Rome.

17. Severo Sarduy provides another description of this place in "El texto devorado: Apuntes para un ensayo sobre *Las virtudes del pájaro solitario* de Juan Goytisolo" (*II Seminario* 3–7), reminding his readers he has also described this meeting place in his novel *Colibrí.*

18. Linda Gould Levine, in "El papel paradójico del SIDA en *Las virtudes del pájaro solitario*" (*II Seminario* 232–44), provides an excellent reading, applying Susan Sontag's ideas of the contradictory values attached to this deathly sickness to Goytisolo's novel. Paul Julian Smith point out, correctly in my view, that "people with AIDS are unlikely to derive much comfort from Goytisolo's description of their predicament. From their perspective, *Las virtudes* can be read as a morbid account of the spectacle of suffering; as an improper attack on a gay community depicted as twittering in a gilded cage; as a misguided attempt to transform physical misfortune into redemptive sacrifice" (*Representing the Other* 212). It certainly can. But comfort may not be all that is needed, or sufficient. I fail to see why Saint John's example of transmuting his physical misfor-

tune into poetry and a celebration of love cannot be a path to follow for some people who suffer greatly. As a local possibility, not a universal prescription, this may work.

19. For the importance of simulation in this novel, following Jean Baudrillard's analyses, see the essential and perceptive study *"Las virtudes del pájaro solitario*: The Death of Symbolic Exchange," by Paul Julian Smith, in his *Representing the Other*, pp. 204–15.

20. These episodes were inspired by the Cuban writer Jorge Ronet's *La mueca de la paloma negra*. For this, and other tracings of correspondence, see Manuel Ruiz Lagos's useful "Del paraíso fingido al jardín del hombre interior: Sobrelectura singular del *Pájaro solitario*" (*II Seminario* 9–37).

21. See, for testimonies about the existence of this treatise, Crisógono de Jesús's detailed biography of Saint John of the Cross in *Vida y obras de San Juan de la Cruz*, 242–44. Apparently, *Propiedades del pájaro solitario* was destroyed by a nun who burned a large quantity of works by Saint John in 1591, to prevent them from falling into the hands of one of his enemies, Father Diego Evangelista. Father Crisógono's text is written with novelistic flair and finds its way into many passages of *Las virtudes*.

22. Ruiz Lagos, in "Pájaros" (186), identifies this character with Goytisolo's great-uncle, Ramón Vives Pastor, who was a bohemian and at one stage of his life had tuberculosis, becoming a persona non grata with his family both for his style of living and his sickness. In *Forbidden Territory* (24) Goytisolo remembers that when he was a child he used the reverse side of the surviving manuscripts of his great-uncle to write his plays, which were then discarded. Goytisolo, by bringing him back to contemplate the destruction of a library, seems to be ritually repaying a private debt.

23. This may explain Goytisolo's admonition to the scholars meeting in Almería to discuss *The Virtues of the Solitary Bird*, when he wrote that "confronted by the Sufi language, by the language of Saint John, and with the language of the *Pájaro*, I honestly believe that the task of uncovering its roots is . . . another way of beating around the bush" (*II Seminario* 1, my translation of "la tarea de buscar sus raíces es . . . otra manera de andarse por las ramas").

24. This was the reason Goytisolo gave me when I asked him why he had selected Savater, among all other possible candidates, for the distinction of being highlighted among the inhabitants of hell.

25. According to *The Encyclopaedia of Islam*, Munkar and Nakir "are the names of the two angels who examine and if necessary punish the dead in their tombs" (vol. seven, 576). The question they pose to the dead is about the identity of Muhammad, and the reply must be that he is the Apostle of Allah. Any

other answer, as those Goytisolo seems ready to provide, will elicit severe and continued beatings from both angels, which will last until the Day of Resurrection, with the exception of Fridays.

26. I offer here a translation closer to the Spanish text than the perfectly acceptable, but more creative, translation by Peter Bush in the published English edition.

27. The question could arise about my position here in presenting Goytisolo's work. Am I the prosecuting attorney, a lawyer for the defense, or the judge? Or a less judgmental analyst? I prefer to think of myself as a skilled technician who enjoys showing others how complex mechanisms work and how they can be tuned for maximum performance.

28. This knowledge has been resisted in Europe, perhaps in part because most scholars do not read Arabic. For an updated version of this issue, see María Rosa Menocal's *The Arabic Role in Medieval Literary History: A Forgotten Heritage.*

29. Al-Arabi's own narrative of his encounters with Averroës in Cordoba and his account of the transfer of Averroës's body from Marrakesh, where he died, to his native Cordoba, are masterful. A Spanish translation can be found in Asín Palacios's *El Islam cristianizado*, 39–41.

30. The translation comes from Annemarie Schimmel's *As Through a Veil: Mystical Poetry of Islam*, 38–39, where she warns that this poem should not be read as a reductionist praise of all religions—as Goytisolo does here—but more as a tribute to Islam's all-encompassing reach.

31. I cannot recommend too strongly the convenience of reading pp. 68-69 of "On the Uses and Disadvantages of History for Life." Despite the slight problem of chronology, this essay contains one the best interpretations of Goytisolo's writing available, as Borges would have put it.

32. I use here the Spanish title because an English translation is still not available as I write this chapter.

33. This adjective, *faithful*, is repeatedly used by H. F. Peters in his biography of Jenny von Westphalen, Marx's wife, *Red Jenny: A Life with Karl Marx*, a book from which Goytisolo appears to have taken a considerable amount of material.

34. The extensive description of Marx and his dwelling on Dean Street in London which Goytisolo includes with few changes in the novel can be found on pp. 251–52 of Robert Payne's *Marx*, another book which apparently was extensively used by Goytisolo in preparing this novel.

35. This party actually took place on 12 October 1864, and the invitation the narrator receives can be found on p. 355 of Payne's *Marx*.

36. The inevitable comparison here is with Mario Vargas Llosa's *Aunt Julia and the Scriptwriter*, a novel of 1977, in which the Peruvian writer alternates chapters containing wildly imaginative radio scripts, written by one of the characters, with other chapters which are autobiographical and realistic. As the novel progresses, both worlds intermingle and eventually reflect each other, raising the sort of questions Brian McHale in *Postmodernist Fiction* (10–11) calls ontological, meaning that the questions in it are not any longer the modernist epistemological questions of what is truth and how do we know the world, but instead which world is this, how many different worlds are there, and which of each person's many selves is acting in them.

BIBLIOGRAPHY

What follows is a list of the works cited in this book, which serves also as a selection of the vast bibliography available on Juan Goytisolo. The bibliography gives the first edition of all the narrative works published by Goytisolo, as well as of his volumes of essays, travel descriptions, and autobiography.

A. Works by Juan Goytisolo

Narrative (Spanish Editions)

Juegos de manos. Barcelona: Destino, 1954.

Duelo en el paraíso. Barcelona: Destino, 1955.

El circo. Barcelona: Destino, 1957.

La resaca. Paris: Librairie Espagnole, 1958.

Fiestas. Barcelona: Destino, 1958.

Para vivir aquí. Buenos Aires: Sur, 1960.

La isla. Barcelona: Seix Barral, 1961.

Fin de fiesta. Tentativas de interpretación de una historia amorosa. Barcelona: Seix Barral, 1962.

Señas de identidad. México: Joaquín Mortiz, 1966. (The second edition of 1969, considerably revised by the author, should be considered the definitive one.)

Reivindicación del conde don Julián. México: Joaquín Mortiz, 1970. There is a critical and indispensable edition by Linda Gould Levine (Madrid: Cátedra, 1985).

Juan sin tierra. Barcelona: Seix Barral, 1975.

Obras completas. 2 vols. Introduction by Pere Gimferrer. Madrid: Aguilar, 1977. (First volume contains *Juegos de manos, Duelo en "El Paraíso," Fiestas,* and *La Resaca.* Second volume contains *Para vivir aquí, La isla, Fin de fiesta, Campos de Níjar, La Chanca, Pueblo en Marcha,* and *El furgón de cola.*)

Makbara. Barcelona: Seix Barral, 1980.

Paisajes después de la batalla. Barcelona: Montesinos, 1982.

Las virtudes del pájaro solitario. Barcelona: Seix Barral, 1988.

La cuarentena. Madrid: Mondadori, 1991.

La saga de los Marx. Barcelona: Mondadori, 1993.

Narrative (English Editions)

Children of Chaos. Trans. Christine Brooke-Rose. London: Macgibbon & Kee, 1958.

The Young Assassins. Trans. John Rust. New York: Knopf, 1959.

Fiestas. Trans. Herbert Weinstock. New York: Knopf, 1960.

Island of Women. Trans. José Yglesias. New York: Knopf, 1962. Same translation published as *Sands of Torremolinos*. London: Cape, 1962.

The Party's Over: Four Attempts to Define a Love Story. Trans. José Yglesias. New York: Grove, 1966.

Marks of Identity. Trans. José Rabassa. New York: Grove, 1969.

Count Julian. Trans. Helen R. Lane. New York: Seaver Books (Viking), 1974.

Juan the Landless. Trans. Helen R. Lane. New York: Seaver Books (Viking), 1977.

Makbara. Trans. Helen R. Lane. New York: Seaver Books (Viking), 1981.

Landscapes after the Battle. Trans. Helen R. Lane. New York: Seaver Books (Viking), 1987.

The Virtues of the Solitary Bird. Trans. Helen Lane. London: Serpent's Tail, 1991.

Quarantine: A Novel. Trans. Peter Bush. Normal, Ill.: Dalkey Archive, 1994.

Other Works (Spanish Editions)

Problemas de la novela. Barcelona: Seix Barral, 1959.

Campos de Níjar. Barcelona: Seix Barral, 1959.

La Chanca. Paris: Librarie Espagnole, 1962.

Pueblo en marcha. Tierras de Manzanillo. Instantáneas de un viaje a Cuba. Paris: Librairie des Editions Espagnoles, 1962.

El furgón de cola. París: Ruedo Ibérico, 1967.

España y los españoles. Barcelona: Lumen, 1979. (First published in Lucerne: Verlag Bucher, 1969. The Spanish edition adds a new concluding chapter.)

Obra inglesa de Blanco White. Buenos Aires: Ediciones Formentor, 1972. (More accessible is the third edition, Barcelona: Seix Barral, 1982.)

Disidencias. Barcelona: Seix Barral, 1977.

Libertad, libertad, libertad. Barcelona: Anagrama, 1978.

El problema del Sahara. Barcelona: Anagrama, 1979.

Crónicas sarracinas. Paris: Ruedo Ibérico, 1982.

Contracorrientes. Barcelona: Montesinos, 1985.

Coto vedado. Barcelona: Seix Barral, 1985.
En los reinos de taifa. Barcelona: Seix Barral, 1986.
Estambul otomano. Barcelona: Planeta, 1989.
Aproximaciones a Gaudí en Capadocia. Madrid: Mondadori, 1990.
Cuaderno de Sarajevo: Anotaciones de un viaje a la barbarie. Madrid: El País, 1993.

Other Works (English Editions)

"Literature Pursued by Politics." *Review of Contemporary Fiction* 4, 2 (1984): 34–38.
The Countryside of Níjar and La Chanca. Trans. Luigi Luccarelli. Plainfield, Ind.: Alembic Press, 1987.
Space in Motion. Trans. by Helen R. Lane. New York: Lumen Books, 1987.
Forbidden Territory. The Memoirs of Juan Goytisolo, 1931–1956. Trans. Peter Bush. San Francisco: North Point Press, 1989.
Realms of Strife. The Memoirs of Juan Goytisolo, 1957–1982. Trans. Peter Bush. San Francisco: North Point Press, 1990.
Saracen Chronicles: A Selection of Literary Essays. London: Quartet Books, 1992.

B. Interviews

Gautier, Marie-Lise Gazarian. "Juan Goytisolo." In *Interviews with Spanish Writers*. Elmwood Park, Ill.: Dalkey Archive Press, 1991. 137–50.
Geist, Anthony L. "An Interview with Juan Goytisolo." *TriQuarterly* 57, 2 (1983): 38–48.
Hernández, José A. "Juan Goytisolo—1975." *MLN* 91 (1976): 337–55.
Ortega, Julio. "An Interview with Juan Goytisolo." *Review of Contemporary Fiction* 4, 2 (1984): 4–19. (Trans. by Joseph Schraibman. Originally appeared in *Texas Quarterly* [Spring 1975].)
Rodríguez Monegal, Emir. "Destrucción de la España sagrada." *Mundo Nuevo*, 12 (June 1967): 44–60.

C. Books: On Goytisolo

Levine, Linda Gould. *Juan Goytisolo: La destrucción creadora*. Mexico: Mortiz, 1976. A seminal study on *Marks of Identity* and *Count Julian*.

Meerts, Christian. *Technique et Vision dans "Señas de identidad" de J. Goytisolo*. Frankfurt am Main: Vittorio Klostermann, 1972. A psychological approach.

Navajas, Gonzalo. *La novela de Juan Goytisolo*. Madrid: SGEL, 1979. A perceptive overview.

Ortega, José. *Juan Goytisolo: Alienación y agresión en* Señas de identidad *y* Reivindicación del conde don Julián. New York: Eliseo Torres, 1972.

Schaefer-Rodríguez, Claudia. *Juan Goytisolo: Del 'realismo crítico' a la utopía*. Madrid: José Porrúa Turanzas, 1984.

Six, Abigail Lee. *Juan Goytisolo: The Case for Chaos*. New Haven: Yale UP, 1990.

Sotomayor, Carmen. *Una lectura orientalista de Juan Goytisolo*. Madrid: Espiral Hispano-Americana, 1990.

Ugarte, Michael. *Trilogy of Treason. An Intertextual Study of Juan Goytisolo*. Columbia, Mo.: U of Missouri P, 1982. Essential.

D. Collections

Anthropos 60–61 (1986). Nine essays on Goytisolo plus a bibliography.

Catálogo: Juan Goytisolo. Almería: Instituto de Estudios Almerienses, 1987.

Escritos sobre Juan Goytisolo. Coloquio en torno a la obra de Juan Goytisolo, Almería 1987. Almería: Instituto de Estudios Almerienses, 1988. Sixteen valuable essays on Goytisolo's work written, among others, by Linda Gould Levine, Annie Perrin, Ahmed Beremdane, Andrés Sánchez Robayna, Manuel Ruiz Lagos, and Julián Ríos.

Juan Goytisolo. Madrid: Espiral / Fundamentos, 1975. Contains an important autobiographical introduction and nine essays by Gonzalo Sobejano, Manuel Durán, J. C. Curuchet, Christian Meerts, Carlos Fuentes, Kessel Schwartz, Mario Vargas Llosa, Severo Sarduy, and José María Castellet.

Juan Goytisolo. Ed. Manuel Ruiz Lagos. Madrid: Fondo de Cultura Hispánica, 1991. Transcriptions of a colloquium dedicated to Goytisolo's work, with the intervention of the author, in Buenos Aires, 2–5 October 1989.

Juan sin Tierra. Madrid: Espiral/Revista 2, 1977. Sixteen essays on *Juan the Landless*, plus an interview with Goytisolo and fragments of a letter by Octavio Paz.

Norte 13 (1972). Four essays on Goytisolo by S. R. Wilson, Kessel Schwartz, Manuel Durán, and Linda Gould Levine.

Review of Contemporary Fiction 4, 2 (1984). Twelve critical essays, plus interviews and selections of Goytisolo's works.

II Seminario Internacional sobre la obra de Juan Goytisolo (Las virtudes del pájaro solitario). Almería: Instituto de Estudios Almerienses, 1989. Sixteen important essays on *The Virtues of the Solitary Bird*.

Voces 1 (1981). Six critical essays, plus three essays by Goytisolo, an interview with him, and an introduction by Pere Gimferrer.

E. Articles and Other Publications on Goytisolo

Alonso Hernández, José Luis. "Para las señas de *Makbara* de Juan Goytisolo." *Co-textes* 5 (1983): 59–106.

Benremdane, Ahmed. "El dialecto marroquí empleado en la obra de Juan Goytisolo: Función y significación." In *Escritos sobre Juan Goytisolo*. 91–98.

Epps, Brad. "The Politics of Ventriloquism: Cava, Revolution and Sexual Discourse in *Conde Julián*." *MLN* 107 (1992): 274–97.

Escudero, Javier. "Del cementerio al infierno de la misericordia: Muerte, espiritualidad y mística erótica en el último Juan Goytisolo (1982–1992)." Diss. University of Virginia, 1992. An excellent study.

Gimferrer, Pere. *"La cuarentena* de Juan Goytisolo." *Vuelta* 17 (April 1993): 11–12.

Kiely, Robert. "The Métro to Apocalypse: *Landscapes After the Battle* by Juan Goytisolo." *The New York Times Book Review*, 14 June 1987, 7.

Levine, Linda Gould. "El papel paradójico del 'Sida' en *Las virtudes del pájaro solitario*." In *II Seminario Internacional sobre la obra de Juan Goytisolo (Las virtudes del pájaro solitario)*. 232–44

López Baralt, Luce. "Juan Goytisolo aprende a reir: Los contextos caribeños de *Makbara* y *Paisajes después de la batalla.*" *Insula*, 468 (1985): 3–4.

Martín, Marina. "Juan Goytisolo en deuda con Américo Castro: *Reivindicación del conde don Julián*." *LP* (1989): 211–23.

Martín Morán, José Manuel. "Instrucciones de vuelo para el *Pájaro solitario*." In *II Seminario Internacional sobre la obra de Juan Goytisolo (Las virtudes del pájaro solitario)*. 98–120.

———. *"Paisajes después de la batalla.* La verdad, la ficción y el vacío." In *Escritos sobre Juan Goytisolo. Coloquio en torno a la obra de Juan Goytisolo, Almería 1987*. 147–167.

Perrin, Annie. "Pour une écriture-lecture-audition: *Makbara* ou la voix retrouvée." *Co-textes* 5 (1983): 41–57.

Pope, Randolph D. "El autorretrato postmoderno de Juan Goytisolo." In *L'autoportrait en Espagne: Littérature & Peinture*. Aix-en-Provence: Publications de l'Université de Provence, 1992. 319–30.

———. "La censura en las primeras novelas de Juan Goytisolo." *España Contemporánea* 3 (1990): 97–104.

———. "The Different Architectures of Metafiction in Juan and Luis Goytisolo." *España Contemporánea* 1 (1988): 145–50.

———. "La hermandad del crimen: Genet examina a Goytisolo." In *Estudios en homenaje a Enrique Ruiz-Fornells*. Juan Fernández Jiménez, José Labrador Herraiz, and Teresa Valdivieso, eds., Erie, Pa.: ALDEEU, 1990. 514–18.

———. "Remembrance and Creative Nostalgia in Juan Goytisolo (and the Misplaced Presence of Rousseau)." In Myron Lichtblau, ed., *La emigración y el exilio en la literatura hispánica del siglo veinte*. Miami: Ediciones Universal, 1988. 13–20.

———. "Theory and Contemporary Autobiographical Writing: The Case of Juan Goytisolo." *Siglo XX/20th Century* 8 (1990–1991) : 87–101.

———. "Writing After the Battle: Juan Goytisolo's Renewal,"in *Literature, the Arts, and Democracy: Spain in the Eighties*, edited by Samuel Amell. London and Toronto: Associated University Presses, 1990. 58–66.

Rogers, Lynne. "*Reivindicación del Conde don Julián:* A Descent into Abjection." *Letras Peninsulares* 3 (1990): 279–91.

Rogmann, Horst. "El contradictorio Juan Goytisolo." *Insula* 31 (October 1976): 1, 12.

Ruiz Lagos, Manuel. "Del paraíso fingido al jardín del hombre interior: Sobrelectura singular del *Pájaro solitario*." In *II Seminario Internacional sobre la obra de Juan Goytisolo (Las virtudes del pájaro solitario)*. 9–37

———. "Pájaros en vuelo a Simorg. Transferencias y metamorfosis textual en un relato de Juan Goytisolo: *Las virtudes del pájaro solitario*." In *Escritos sobre Juan Goytisolo. Coloquio en torno a la obra de Juan Goytisolo, Almería 1987*. 171–228.

Sánchez Robayna, Andrés. "Góngora y la novela: 'Don Julián', de Juan Goytisolo." *Sintaxis*, 12–13 (Fall 1986–Winter 1987): 50–58.

Sarduy, Severo. "El texto devorado. Apuntes para un ensayo sobre *Las virtudes del pájaro solitario*," in *II Seminario Internacional sobre la obra de Jaun Goytisolo (Las virtudes del pájaro solitario)*. Almería: Instituto de Estudios Almerienses, 1989. 3–7

Schwartz, Kessel. "Juan Goytisolo, *Juan sin tierra*, and the Anal Aesthetic." *Hispania* 62 (1979): 9–19.

Sieburth, Stephanie. "Reading and Alienation in Goytisolo's *Reivindicación del conde don Julián.*"*Anales de la Literatura Española Contemporánea* 8 (1983): 83–93.

Smith, Paul Julian. "Homosexual Desire in Goytisolo's Trilogy of Treason." In *Laws of Desire: Questions of Homosexuality in Spanish Writing and Film, 1960–1990.* Oxford: Clarendon Press, 1992. 55–90.

———. *Representing the Other: 'Race', Text, and Gender in Spanish and Spanish American Narrative.* Oxford: Clarendon Press, 1992.

Sobejano, Gonzalo. "Don Julián, iconoclasta de la literatura patria." *Camp de l'arpa*, 43/44 (April/May 1977): 7–14.

Spires, Robert. "Process as Product: *Juan sin Tierra.*" In *Beyond the Metafictional Mode. Directions in the Modern Spanish Novel.* Lexington: The UP of Kentucky, 1984. 72–88.

Ugarte, Michael. "Juan Goytisolo: Unruly Disciple of Américo Castro." *Journal of Spanish Studies: Twentieth Century* 7, 3 (1979): 353–64.

Wood, Michael. "O Tempora! O Moors!" [Review of *Count Julian.*] *The New York Review of Books*, 8 August 1974, 40–41.

F. Other Studies

Abelove, Henry, Michèle Aina Barale, and David M. Halperin, eds. *The Lesbian and Gay Studies Reader.* New York: Routledge, 1993.

Almansi, Guido, ed. *Lewis Carroll: Photos and Letters to his Child Friends.* Parma: Franco Maria Ricci, 1975.

Asín Palacios, Miguel. *La escatología musulmana en la Divina Comedia.* Madrid: RAE, 1919. Translated as *Islam and the Divine Comedy.* Trans. H. Sunderland. New York: E. P. Dutton, 1926.

———. *El Islam cristianizado. Estudio del "sufismo" a través de Abenarabi de Murcia.* 2nd. ed. Madrid: Hiperión, 1981.

Attar, Farid Ud-Din. *The Conference of the Birds.* Trans. Afkam Darbandi and Dick Davis. New York: Penguin, 1984.

Barrero Pérez, Oscar. *La novela existencial española de posguerra.* Madrid: Gredos, 1987.

Barthes, Roland. *Writing Degree Zero.* Trans. by Annette Lavers and Colin Smith. Preface by Susan Sontag. New York: Hill and Wang, 1968.

Carrouges, Michel. *Soldier of the Spirit. The Life of Charles de Foucauld.* Trans. Marie-Christine Hellin. New York: Putnam, 1956.

Castellet, José María. *La hora del lector*. Barcelona: Seix Barral, 1957.

Cela, Camilo José. *Viaje a la Alcarria*. Madrid: Revista de Occidente, 1948. Translated as *Journey to the Alcarria*. Trans. Frances M. López-Morillas. Madison: U of Wisconsin P, 1964.

Deleuze, Gilles, and Félix Guattari. *Anti-Oedipus. Capitalism and Schizophrenia*. Preface by Michel Foucault. Trans. Robert Hurley, Mark Seem, and Helen R. Lane. Minneapolis: U of Minnesota P, 1983.

———. *A Thousand Plateaus: Capitalism and Schizophrenia*. Trans. Brian Massumi. Minneapolis. U of Minnesota P, 1987.

Edelman, Lee. "Tearooms and Sympathy, or, The Epistemology of the Water Closet." Eds. Henry Abelove et al. New York: Routledge, 1993. 553–74.

Ferres, Antonio, and Armando López Salinas. *Caminando por Las Hurdes*. Barcelona: Seix Barral, 1960.

Fraser, Ronald. *Blood of Spain: An Oral History of the Spanish Civil War*. New York: Pantheon Books, 1979.

Garber, Marjorie. *Vested Interests: Cross-Dressing & Cultural Anxiety*. New York and London: Routledge, 1992.

Genet, Jean. *The Thief's Journal*. Trans. Bernard Frechtman. New York: Grove, 1964.

Gernsheim, Helmut. *Lewis Carroll, Photographer*. New York: Chanticleer Press, 1949.

Gibbon, Edward. *Memoirs of My Life*. Ed. Betty Radice. London: Penguin Books, 1984.

Gil Casado, Pablo. *La novela social española (1920–1971)*. 2nd. ed. Barcelona: Seix Barral, 1973.

Gómez-Martínez, José Luis. *Américo Castro y el origen de los españoles: Historia de una polémica*. Madrid: Gredos, 1975.

Hamilton, Elizabeth. *The Desert My Dwelling Place. A Study of Charles de Foucauld, 1858–1916*. London: Hodder and Stoughton, 1968.

Harvey, David. *The Condition of Postmodernity: An Enquiry into the Origins of Cultural Change*. Oxford: Basil Blackwell, 1989.

Heath, Peter. *The Philosopher's Alice*. New York: St. Martin's Press, 1974.

Higginbotham, Virginia. *Spanish Film Under Franco*. Austin: U of Texas P, 1988.

Ibn Al-Arabi, Muhyiddin. *The Seals of Wisdom*. Oxford: Concord Grove Press, 1983.

James, William. *The Varieties of Religious Experience. A Study in Human Nature*. Harmondsworth: Penguin Books, 1982.

Juan de la Cruz, San. *Vida y obras de San Juan de la Cruz*. With a biography by Crisógono de Jesús, O.C.D. 5th ed. Madrid: Biblioteca de Autores Cristianos, 1964.

Lacan, Jacques. *Écrits: A Selection*. Trans. Alan Sheridan. New York: Norton, 1977.

Lamartine, Alphonse de. *Oeuvres Poétiques*. Paris: Gallimard, 1965.

Lawrence, T. E. *Seven Pillars of Wisdom: A Triumph*. Garden City, N.Y.: Doubleday, Doran, 1935.

López Baralt, Luce. *San Juan de la Cruz y el Islam*. 2nd. ed. Madrid: Hiperión, 1990.

Machado, Manuel. *Antología*. Barcelona: Plaza y Janés, 1974.

Mannheim, Karl. *Ideology and Utopia: An Introduction to the Sociology of Knowledge*. Trans. Louis Wirth and Edward Shils. New York: Harcourt, Brace & World, 1965.

Matthews, Herbert L. *The Yoke and the Arrows: A Report on Spain*. New York: Braziller, 1957.

McHale, Brian. *Postmodernist Fiction*. New York: Methuen, 1987.

Menéndez Pidal, Ramón. "La leyenda de cómo se perdió España." In *España y su historia*. Madrid: Minotauro: 1957. 239–71.

Menocal, María Rosa. *The Arabic Role in Medieval Literary History: A Forgotten Heritage*. Philadelphia: U of Pennsylvania P, 1987.

Nietzsche, Friedrich. "On the Uses and Disadvantages of History for Life." In *Untimely Meditations*. Trans. R. J. Hollingdale. Cambridge and New York: Cambridge UP, 1983. 57–123.

Payne, Robert. *Marx*. New York: Simon and Schuster, 1968.

Payne, Stanley G. *Falange: A History of Spanish Fascism*. Stanford: Stanford UP, 1961.

Percival, José María. "Asco y asquerosidad del morisco según los apologistas cristianos del Siglo de Oro." *La Torre* 4 (1990): 21–47.

Peters, H. F. *Red Jenny: A Life with Karl Marx*. New York: St. Martin's Press, 1986.

Pope, Randolph D. "Camilo José Cela." In *European Writers: The Twentieth Century*. New York: Scribners, 1990. 3105–29.

Rubin, Gayle S. "Thinking Sex: Notes for a Radical Theory of the Politicis of Sexuality." In Henry Abelone, Michèle Aina Barale, and David M. Halperin, eds., *The Lesbian and Gay Studies Reader*. New York: Routledge, 1993. 3–44.

Sartre, Jean-Paul. *The Words*. Trans. Bernard Frechtman. New York: Vintage Books, 1981. (Originally published in French as *Les Mots* [Paris: Gallimard, 1964].)

Schimmel, Annemarie. *As Through a Veil: Mystical Poetry in Islam*. New York: Columbia UP, 1982.

Schulte, Henry F. *The Spanish Press, 1470–1966: Print, Power, and Politics*. Urbana: U of Illinois P, 1968.

Sobejano, Gonzalo. *Novela española de nuestro tiempo (en busca del tiempo perdido)*. 2nd ed. Madrid: Prensa Española, 1975.

Underhill, Evelyn. *Mysticism: A Study in the Nature and Development of Man's Spiritual Consciousness*. New York: Dutton, 1961.

Venturi, Robert, Denise Scott Brown, and Steven Izenour. *Learning from Las Vegas*. Rev. ed. Cambridge, Mass.: The MIT Press, 1977.

Weinberg, Martin S., Colin J. Williams, and Douglas W. Pryor. *Dual Attraction: Understanding Bisexuality*. New York: Oxford UP, 1994.

Wilson, Jeremy. *Lawrence of Arabia: The Authorized Biography of T. E. Lawrence*. New York: Atheneum, 1990.

INDEX